WHAT YOU SHOULD KNOW
ABOUT CONTRACTS

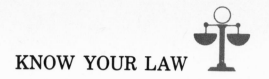

KNOW YOUR LAW

What You Should Know About CONTRACTS

ROBERT A. FARMER & ASSOCIATES

New York

Published by ARCO PUBLISHING COMPANY, Inc.
219 Park Avenue South, New York, N. Y. 10003
Copyright © Robert A. Farmer, 1969
Library of Congress Catalog Card Number 69-11145
Standard Book Number 668-01826-7
Printed in the United States of America

Contents

Preface

A contract is an agreement, enforceable by law, between two or more parties. Although the content, form, and subject matter of contracts vary widely, every contract involves the exchange of something of value between the participating parties.

Contracts are essential to modern society. Not only do they form the backbone of commercial transactions—they also play an important part in the lives of private individuals. Everything from the purchase of a snow shovel or railroad ticket to the execution of a mortgage necessitates some sort of contract. The importance and number of contracts in which every individual invariably becomes involved demands that he be familiar with the fundamental characteristics and rules of these agreements. Curiously, most of us are not. Many people realize too late that a better knowledge of the legal obligations arising out of a transaction which they naively or foolishly entered into would have prevented much loss and grief.

The contract is a creation of the law. In the course of the last several hundred years judges and legislators have established the rules and conditions which govern all aspects of contracts. Although there are many complex, archaic, and inconsistent principles affecting contracts, a careful and rational consideration of the contract and its ground rules will help the layman be more effective in his daily business encounters—regardless of whether these encounters involve only a few dollars or several thousand. This book is a simple, yet complete discussion of all types of contracts. Even though it should be evident that no introductory book can supplant sound legal advice, it is hoped that this volume will help the reader avoid foolish and often costly mistakes which make professional aid necessary, and may lead to expensive litigation.

1. Introduction to the Contract

When two or more parties enter into a legally binding agreement for the purpose of exchanging objects of value or securing the performance of acts or services, a contract is created.

The range of situations in which the contract is a useful or even essential instrument is indeed broad. Whenever people wish to insure their expectations and to make obligations and duties concrete, a contract is used. A contract between men signifies both have given their word, and a bargain has been struck, a bargain which cannot later be revoked or escaped without risking penalties imposed by a court. In earlier times a man's promise carried only the weight of his reputation or of his adversary's strength; today, promises, when they assume contractual form, have the force of law behind them. The form is flexible and has many varieties. As dealings between men become more complex and pervasive, the institution of contract has changed to aid and contain these dealings. A contract may be written or oral. It may encompass any object or activity which is not illegal, or unsuitable for enforcement by the courts.

The omnipresent nature of contracts is most apparent in the commercial world: no prudent businessman enters into a transaction without the execution of a contract between the parties to insure performance. The formal written agreement promising the transfer of thousands of acres of land as well as the sale of ten shares of securities by telephone are both enforceable contracts. Form is important only to the extent that the parties must observe a minimum number of technical, legal rules. The crucial factor is that both parties should realize that their agreement imparts a legal obligation to supply whatever has been agreed to, and that the courts will enforce the promises and penalize a refusal to perform.

The nonbusiness individual most frequently encounters the contract when he acquires goods or services from the business world.

The purchase of an airplane ticket, a plot of land, an insurance policy, and the execution of a mortgage—all involve the formation of a contract. But while businessmen generally realize the legal effect of a contract, the same is not true of those outside the commercial sphere. Drastic results may follow the uninformed or hasty action of any individual entering a contract. When trouble involving a contract occurs, the man on the street often loses both money and his respect for the legal profession—perhaps even for the law.

Although the law of contract may be flexible in situations of acute injustice, it cannot vary to the extent of becoming undependable or capricious. In effect, this frequently results in penalizing the careless actions of uneducated citizens. Laws must be fixed, explicit, and shaped by the mores of the time; a man must be presumed to realize the legal effect of his actions. Thus, when an uninformed individual violates the law, most often the court, not he, prevails. One answer to this regrettable lack of communication between the legal profession and the public is to render legal institutions and rules understandable to laymen.

Rules which may at first appear to be technical, inflexible, or unreasonable in contract law are usually both rational and necessary. To be understood and appreciated, however, the rules must be seen as part of a complete body of law developed through centuries. With only occasional lapses and antiquated rules, contract law has proven to be a workable and essentially sound institution. If the reader can perceive that structure, even vaguely, his understanding of contract law will be made much easier.

Origin and Early Development

Let us begin to uncover this branch of the law by examining the origin of contracts. Why was the contract developed and why has it remained useful to society for centuries? Why is it necessary?

Men have undoubtedly made bargains since the beginning of civilization, and when the exchanges were executed immediately, the trade in itself offered sufficient satisfaction for both parties. However, when such transactions ceased to be simultaneous, complications arose.

For example, suppose that in June, Rancher Smith wants to trade his horse for forty bushels of Farmer Jones's wheat, but Farmer Jones will not harvest his wheat for many months. How can Smith be sure that, when harvest time comes, he will receive the wheat in exchange for the horse he handed over to Jones in June? In a world without formal contracts and courts to enforce them, Smith could be in for a difficult time if Jones refuses to honor the bargain. If Rancher Smith were physically stronger than Farmer Jones and willing to risk battle, he might be able to enforce performance. Or, he might try to reason with Jones, but this could well come to nothing. Therefore, without courts, Smith has only his own strength, or Jones's honesty, to depend upon.

With the appearance of contracts enforced by courts, Rancher Smith would find himself in a considerably better position. If he had been able to induce Farmer Jones to sign a written document in June stating that Jones would deliver forty bushels of wheat to Smith at harvest time in return for Smith's horse in June, Smith could go before the court and ask that Jones be required to deliver the forty bushels of wheat.

What, then, has Rancher Smith gained from the introduction

of contracts and courts? First, he need not make immediate bargains; he can secure the performance of things he desires months or years in advance. Second, he can depend upon the courts to enforce his bargain, rather than upon his own strength or Farmer Jones's honesty. Third, Smith now has several safe options as to the way to proceed with his bargain: he can give his horse now in return for Jones's promise of wheat in the future, or Smith can promise to give Jones the horse at harvest time if the latter assures him of delivery of the wheat after harvest.

Thus, the existence of contracts and courts assures people of fair dealing, allowing them to depend upon others' promises of future performance. Contract law is especially important to businesses, facilitating their entering into and expanding transactions with other firms.

These two worlds of pre- and post-contracts and courts correspond roughly to actual historical periods. Contracts, and courts ready to enforce their provisions, evolved in England during the twelfth and thirteenth centuries. The commercial renaissance which took place at the beginning of the thirteenth century demanded a new, enlightened legal system. Coercion could no longer serve as an effective method for enforcing bargains between men. If a merchant agreed to supply goods, others depended on him, and this mutual dependence within the trading, commercial society required that each man be held to his word. Not surprisingly, the first courts enforcing promises developed within these trading communities—in ports, and at fairs, where the merchants themselves sat to judge their fellows, using the traditional trade standards which had grown up among them as law.

Later, the ruling monarch established a nationwide system of courts, where from the various local customs, King Henry II's justices formulated a body of law common to the entire kingdom. These courts applied a system of law arising from precedent, rather than statute; hence, the term "common law" was used.

It should be noted that American contract law closely resembles its British counterpart and, as we shall see in the following chapters, neither has changed greatly from English common law of the fourteenth century.

Nearly all promises between individuals were enforceable by the fourteenth century. Unfortunately, as the common law system aged, it became more rigid and lost much of its flexibility; courts and lawyers grew increasingly pretentious and protective of their own narrow interests. New situations arose, but the law did not change. Even today, portions of contract law are hindered by centuries-old rules which courts have never altered, although they result in inconvenience or injustice. An interesting example is the seventeenth century Statute of Frauds which requires that certain types of contracts be written to be enforceable. Prior to the passage of the statute, nearly all promises, written and oral, were enforceable. But it was easy and not uncommon for men to lie about oral contracts, and courts wanted to be spared the difficulty of deciding which party was telling the truth.

Land was particularly important in the early centuries of English common law; being almost the sole source of wealth, it was passed down within a family for generations. Because men wished to be absolutely sure that land was transferred correctly and honestly, with very few exceptions a written contract was essential to insure another's performance in accordance with his promise.

For example, A, a cheat and villain, owned Blackacre farm which he agreed to sell to B for $1,000. No written contract was signed, but B turned over the $1,000 to A who then refused to give B the property. According to the Statute of Frauds, a court would not award B the farm because there was no written contract. Even today, B would have only a slightly better chance of winning, since this section of the statute dealing with land transfers still exists in almost every jurisdiction. In fact, in most states the present statute duplicates the law of England in 1677.

This, then, is an example of the occasional flaw—the trap for the unwary—in the law of contract, which is the result of the requirements of an ancient and obsolete society. When the statute was passed, the importance of land as wealth in English society made the rule reasonable. Today, however, wealth can take many forms, with the result that property is transferred much more readily. No longer is it essential or even reasonable that real estate remain in one family for centuries. But the rule remains to trap the careless and ignorant. This section of the statute does have some value: the courts are still interested in making sure that men's bargains are recorded; written agreements are much more difficult to alter, and a man signing a document is more apt to realize he is obligating himself to do what he promises. Yet when the rule requiring written contracts is enforced strictly, occasional injustice results. Undoubtedly, if nothing but injustice were done by enforcing it, the rule would have been changed long ago. But the law is conservative and slow to change to a new and untried rule—especially if some good is done by an old legal form.

What happens when injustice is done? Are there no exceptions to the legal rules? And if the law is slow to change, then how does change come about?

First, in individual cases, exceptions have been developed to take care of those circumstances in which value inequity would result if a rule were to be interpreted strictly.

In the land transfer case cited, although B could not get the land, he might get his money back, plus compensation, if he suffered any other damages; i.e., if he bought twenty head of cattle to graze on the farm and had to sell them at a loss. A might then be liable for the amount of that loss.

Second, in many instances, the state laws of the U.S. have developed exceptions for these so-called "hard cases." At least one state court says that partial performance by one party makes an oral contract for the sale of land enforceable. Thus, in the above instance, since B's payment of the purchase price is partial performance, the court would require A to transfer the farm.

Third, when the courts decide (usually on the basis of a number of cases which have had undesirable results when the old rule was applied) that the old law should be changed or abolished rather than avoided through developing exceptions, a number of methods are used to effect such an alteration.

The contract law applied within the U.S. comes from many sources. We have tacitly assumed, up until now, that it has come from one source—old English common law. While many state laws governing contracts do stem directly from that body of rules, important changes have been made by the legislatures. Three examples will suffice to illustrate the usual sources of change:

1. The highest state court may simply decide that a particular rule is no longer applicable and state flatly that the common law is henceforth changed. This is rarely done in a single step with open and frank language, but is often accomplished in a series of small and barely noticeable steps—perhaps by the gradual creation of an exception to a rule until the exception, rather than the rule, becomes the law.

2. The state legislature may pass a law which changes or abolishes the old common law. The courts must follow this new law unless it is unconstitutional. This is indeed a frequent source of change in the law of contracts, a recent example being the adoption of the Uniform Commercial Code by the great majority of U.S. state legislatures. The code, as we shall see, changes many common law contract rulings, particularly in the commercial area.

3. Federal laws, which include the U.S. Constitution, decisions of the Supreme Court, statutes passed by Congress, and proclamations issued by the President, as well as rulings by a host of other regulatory and administrative agencies, such as the Interstate Commerce Commission, Federal Trade Commission etc., may change the state law of contracts. Determining when and which federal laws overrule or alter state contract laws is a difficult and complex process and will not concern us.

However, this important source of change in the law must at least be mentioned in our preliminary discussion.

It is possible then, to alter the laws of contract to fit new situations and to avoid the injustices of old rules. That the contract has for centuries remained an essential device to order and regulate transactions between individuals is remarkable. Contracts might not unreasonably be called the lubricant of society. As business, commerce, and individual bargains and promises have expanded, the institution of contract law regulating them has kept pace. If a new type of bargain between men arises, for example, as the insurance contract has over the last half-century—a contractual form to contain the agreement is developed and the courts enforce it.

The body of this book attempts to show the relevance of contracts to the layman, to acquaint him with the elements that are necessary to the proper formation of a contract, and, most important, to make him aware of what happens when something goes wrong with a contract in which he is involved.

2. Requirements for a Valid Contract
Proper Parties

A BASIC element of the contract is that it be entered into by persons. A *person*, for the purpose of contract law, may encompass many things. It can, for example, include a corporation. A corporation, which certainly is not a living being, is recognized as capable of entering into a binding contract with human beings and even other corporations. This is how you become obligated to the phone company. By accepting their service, you enter into a contract whereby you are obligated to pay the bill when it is submitted.

Similarly, a partnership can enter into a contract. The law recognizes a group of people in business as one person capable of binding itself to the terms of an agreement with any other capable person. It does not single out the partners and designate them separately; rather, it views them as a unit, although one or more partners may be authorized by the other partners to enter into contracts for, and in the name of, the partnership.

The Minor

Strangely enough, while the law designates as persons many arrangements which have no human characteristics, it does not recognize many human beings as legal persons. One example is

17

the minor. Thus, in common law, a minor's promise could be voided by him if and when he desired. However, the acts of the adult with whom he contracted could be enforced against the adult by the *infant*.

An infant is not necessarily a baby. At law, an infant is one who has not yet attained the age of twenty-one. There is no legal difference between an infant two years old and one who is twenty. In a few states, one is considered a legal infant until the day preceding his twenty-first birthday.

Although parents have the right to wages earned by an infant and are also entitled to an infant's services, a parent is not liable for the contractual obligations of his child. Thus, if Peter, age fifteen, has entered into a contract with the Acme Building Management Corp. to wash floors, and Peter refuses to wash floors, neither he nor his father can be sued for breach of contract.

The law does not call the contract totally void; the contract is binding on both parties, except that the infant has an option to withdraw from his contracted liability. The infant may choose not to fulfill his promised performance, and the law will not require him to do so.

The law does not forbid the infant from entering into contractual arrangements. It gives him the option to back out of his promise. Thus, if Peter has hired Mr. Smith to paint his car, Peter may withdraw from the agreement, even though it fulfilled all the legal formalities of a contract.

Responsibility in certain transactions, however, cannot be avoided by the infant. If a minor obtains food, clothing, and other necessities under contract, he is generally held liable to the supplier for them. Thus, if Peter went into March's Clothing Store and purchased a shirt and pants on credit, he would have to pay for them. With this exception however, within the entire period of minority, the infant can avoid contractual liabilities. He is not capable of ratifying a contract until he reaches majority. Thus, if Peter enters into a contract with an adult, he could ratify the contract when he reaches twenty-one. But if upon turning twenty-one he fails to disaffirm the contract, he would become liable. Thus, in order for the contract to become "nonvoidable," the minor must reach a majority age.

However, the law requires that if the infant accepts the benefits of the contract, he must accept its detriments as well. When he avoids the contract, he must return anything given him by the other party or be liable for the value of his performance. For example, Peter was to perform services under the contract and has not done so, but he has received advances; Peter must therefore return the advance stipends. If Peter was given $100 to do fifty hours of work, and he only performed twenty-five hours, he would be entitled to $50 and would have to return the other $50.

When the infant has completely parted with any goods received from the other party and has disaffirmed the contract, most courts relieve the infant of any liability. However, some courts say that if there are any goods still in possession of the minor at the time he disaffirms the contract, these goods must be returned to the other contracting party. Thus, if Peter contracted to buy 200 baseball bats, which he received and sold, then disaffirmed the contract after having spent the money, he would not be liable for either the return of the bats or their value. If he had sold only 100 at the point of disapproval, Peter would have to return the other 100. The result in these cases seems inequitable to the party who contracted with the minor, yet this is the price which must be paid if society's laws are to fully protect those incapable of realizing the full effect of their acts, those who are the weakest in society—children.

When credit for necessities is given to the infant personally, he is the only one liable to the creditor. The infant's parents or guardian cannot be held liable for supplying necessities to the infant if they are given directly to him.

The meaning of "necessities" varies with the particular facts of each case. At common law, such things as firearms, horses, and certain types of jewelry have all been considered necessities. American courts have regarded such items as food, clothing, dental and medical expenses, and funeral expenses for a member of the immediate family as necessities and their value recoverable from a minor. In some recent cases even automobiles were considered necessities, and the courts allowed recovery.

Another infant necessity is housing. Once the minor has made use of housing under the terms of a contract, he is bound to pay rent or other compensation for its use. If Peter has entered into a contract to lease an apartment for one year, and three months later he decided to avoid the contract, Peter remains liable for three months' rent. But the landlord cannot sue for the other nine months' rent because Peter's promise as a minor is voidable.

Under old law, only a basic education—such as learning a specific trade—was considered essential. A college, private, or professional school education was not considered necessary. Today, however, the great importance of higher education moves many courts to allow compensation to colleges supplying education to minors. Thus, anything which the infant needs to maintain a normal existence may be considered a necessity. This is not to say that courts consider all types of clothing necessary to an infant. Items considered necessities are evaluated in each particular situation as it arises.

When the infant is adequately supplied with the necessities of food, clothing, and shelter by a parent or legal guardian, anyone else supplying the infant with the same items cannot claim compensation for necessities. An infant could in that case avoid the contract. The creditor has the burden of proving that the goods which he provided were necessities of life. If Peter orders certain articles of clothing from Jones' Department Store, and Peter is living at home, the store must prove to the court that the clothes Peter ordered were necessary to his existence and had not already been supplied by Peter's parents. Even if on entering a contract, a minor lies, claiming that he is twenty-one, the transaction is avoidable. Although the adult party with whom the infant has been trading has relied upon false information, he cannot hold the minor to the terms of the contract.

If Peter has agreed with Mr. Smith, an adult, to buy certain goods, and he takes the goods and resells them prior to avoiding the contract, Peter is not bound by the terms of the contract, even though he has given Mr. Smith false identification showing that he was twenty-one. In some states, however, a minor doing business by false representation may be bound to the terms of the contract. Where an infant who has misrepresented his age does not avoid the contract, but seeks relief because of the other party's breach, the minor cannot use his infancy in order to obtain an advantageous position. The defrauded adult may here avoid the contract.

The reasoning that some courts employ to hold the infant liable when he fraudulently misrepresents his age is that a minor is liable for the *torts* (wrongs or injuries) that he has committed; and misrepresentation in a contractual relationship should not be treated differently than any other tort. Throughout the history of law, an infant has been able to avoid all contractual obligations, yet he has been held liable for any damages caused by his willful, *tortious* (injurious) conduct. Some states allow the wronged party to sue for misrepresentation, but such actions can be brought only if the minor has lied about his age. Furthermore, the adult must prove to the court that the lie told him was reasonable. A ten-year old's false identification showing his age as twenty-one would not form the basis of an action.

A parent's liability for the contract of his child depends upon the particular situation. If a minor contracts to purchase articles of necessity which his parents have refused or neglected to buy, the parents, in most cases, are liable for the infant's obligation. It is the parents' duty to provide necessities for their children. When the child acts for his parent, fulfilling the parent's duty, he acts as the parent's agent, and this binds the parent to the contract on the principle of agency law. Where a parent is not under legal obligation to provide the particular goods for the infant, and the latter is not acting as an agent for the parent, as a rule the parent is not bound by the contractual obligations of the infant.

In most states, an infant cannot bring a legal action in his own name. The action must be brought by a representative called *a next friend,* who may be a parent, relative, guardian, or another adult appointed by the court for the purpose of the litigation. As we saw, a minor is not a legal person in the law's eyes and, consequently, he can not sue in a court of law. The parent or guardian generally has the duty to appear and defend an infant when he is being sued. The court will appoint a *guardian ad litem* (guardian for litigation) for the infant if there are no parents or other legal guardians. A guardian ad litem is a person appointed to act in the child's best interests for purposes of the case. Without a parent's or guardian's consent, an infant cannot admit liability to an act charged.

The Married Woman

At common law, a married woman could not bind herself to a contract during the life of her husband. Widows and unmarried women were not under the same restriction. When a woman married, any contract liabilities she had prior to the marriage were assumed by her husband. Thus, if Marsha was liable for the cost of dresses that she had bought under a contract, upon marriage to Joe, the liability for payment would become Joe's.

Under certain circumstances, the married woman could become liable for her contractual promises, principally where she agreed to render personal services. For example, if Marsha (after marriage) agreed to teach in the New York City school system, but decided to breach the contract, she, and not her husband, would be liable for performance or damages. More than likely, a court would not force Marsha to perform. (A basic rule of law is that performance under personal service contracts cannot be enforced.) Marsha would be liable for damages measured by the costs incurred by the school system in getting a new teacher.

At common law, any property that the wife owned before marriage became the husband's, and any property in which the wife had an interest, or was to have an interest, also became the husband's.

This system of denying the wife property rights was slowly revised by courts and legislatures. At first, the wife was given limited rights, usually a beneficiary's interest with the husband holding the legal interest; he could not destroy or sell the property without her approval. Modern statutes have improved the wife's position, giving her the ability to hold complete and separate interest in property in which the husband has no rights at all.

Quite a few jurisdictions prohibit or limit a wife's contracting with her husband. This is so because the law desires to avoid disputes within the family unit. A few jurisdictions prohibit any contractual relationship between husband and wife, while others forbid only certain kinds of contracts between partners in marriage. Some states prohibit the husband and wife from entering into a partnership agreement. In community property states, such as Arizona, California, and New Mexico, the husband is considered the administrator of all community property.

Since the policy of avoiding intrafamily conflict is not present, and because these agreements are very useful, some contracts between husbands and wives are valid. Thus, separation agreements between husband and wife are perfectly valid, but an agreement on the distribution of the property in their estate must be limited to the property settlement. The contract cannot involve promotion of the divorce which, in the eyes of the law, is immoral and contrary to public policy. For example, Judy and Jim agree that when they are divorced, the house and its contents will go to Judy, and the money in the savings account will go to Jim. The court will look upon this as a private property settlement and will generally allow it in separation or divorce proceedings. However, if the agreement states that Jim will pay Judy $500 for Judy's consent to a divorce, the court will void the contract as being contrary to public policy.

As long as the court is satisfied that the settlement is a fair one and was not procured by fraud or duress, it will generally honor the agreement and incorporate the terms into the divorce settlement. Settlement agreements may include a number of things: the wife's allowance; family support; cost of the divorce litigation; custody of the children, and any division of property.

The Insane

An insane person cannot make a contract. Generally speaking, in order for the contract to be void or voidable by the insane party, the contract must have been formed while the party was legally insane and did not know the nature, purpose, or effect of the transaction in which he became involved.

For example, if John is subject to periods of mental illness, but during a lucid period he enters into a contract, a later attack of mental illness will not be sufficient grounds for avoiding his performance under contract. But if the contract was made by John during a period when he was psychotic, the contract can be void even though John may later recover from the mental illness.

The formal, legal reason for allowing an insane person to avoid a contract is a lack of mutuality in the contract. If one party to the contract is mentally incompetent, there cannot be assent of the two minds, because one is incapable of rational agreement.

The law has always maintained that the insane cannot enter into contracts, convey property by deed, or conduct any commercial transaction, such as giving a note or borrowing money. Courts have held that anyone entering into a contract with an insane person, with prior knowledge that the person is insane, is guilty of fraud or deceit and, therefore, he cannot invoke the court's aid under the contract.

Normally a contract in which one party is insane will not be set aside as void, but may be voidable by the insane party. That is to say, the insane party or his guardian can have it declared invalid. The burden of proving the mental illness which created a lack of understanding falls entirely upon the mentally ill person or his guardian. Although the contract is voidable by the insane individual, it also may be ratified by him during a lucid period. For example, if John enters into a contract while suffering from mental illness, but one week later, during a lucid period, he reaffirms the contract or takes some action, such as receiving or making payment under the contract, the original agreement is valid (or in some instances, a new contract may have been formed).

If the insane individual is placed under guardianship, the guardian can usually ratify the contract on behalf of the deranged individual. However, some courts have held that where the contracting party remains mentally ill, the guardian cannot ratify the contract.

As in the case of an infant, the other party to the contract does not have power to avoid the contract.

However, some courts have taken a different position as far as contracts with the mentally ill are concerned. They have held that so long as no fraud accompanied the transaction, and no undue advantage was taken of the insane individual, and the other party did not know of his mental illness, there is no reason that the contract should not be dissolved—especially if the promises of both parties are still largely unperformed.

3. Requirements for a Valid Contract
The Offer

AN OFFER is a proposal to engage in some type of conduct, made in return for a promise or an act by another. A contract is formed when an offer is accepted. The party accepting an offer is called the *offeree*, and the one making it is called the *offeror*.

The following are examples of an offer: "I will pay you five dollars for that shirt," or "I promise to deliver ten pounds of potatoes if you promise to pay me ten cents per pound." Generally, the offer may contain any terms which the offeror considers desirable to the contractual performance.

Implied Offers

The offer can be expressed in words, by conduct, or other means which communicate a contractual intent or desire to another person. Neither words nor writing is necessary; the mere act of handing a dollar to the ticket seller at the local movie house constitutes an offer to buy a ticket.

An offer must contain a promise, expressing an intent to enter into a contract. "I will sell my car to you on Friday for $500" is an offer; while "I would like to sell my car on Friday for $500" is only a statement of hope or desire, and does not constitute an offer from which a contract may be formed.

A party who states that he cannot sell a certain automobile for less than $1,000 is not making an offer. Again, he is only engaging in hopeful and speculative conversation which as a general rule, does not constitute an offer. To qualify as an offer, a statement must be explicit, tendered to a named or identifiable party with contractual intent. Moreover, the statement cannot be too vague; it must contain definite terms.

A preliminary negotiation, a feeler, or a statement of intention to enter into a discussion is not an offer. "I think I will sell my Cape Cod cottage before the winter," falls into the above category and cannot be considered an offer. It is merely a statement of intention. If the listener responds that he would like to buy the Cape Cod cottage, no contract would result.

Advertisements

In the absence of special circumstances, an ordinary newspaper advertisement is not an offer, but only a proposal to negotiate, or a request to the potential customer to make an offer for the advertised goods. However, if the advertisement uses words of promise which are meant to have a binding effect upon the advertiser, an offer results. For example "We will give $10 to anyone who uses our hair tonic and has not turned blonde within 30 days." This is an offer which can be accepted by the reader.

The same rules that are applicable to advertisements in newspapers and magazines can be applied to prices and advertisements in catalogues. If the catalogue advertisements are accompanied by words stating that quantities of the goods are limited and prices subject to change without notice, the advertisements may be taken merely as requests to make offers or to negotiate—not offers to make a contract. Therefore, they cannot bind the advertiser.

Auction Bids

Usually a bid at an auction is an offer and not acceptance of an offer. When the auctioneer's gavel falls, there is an acceptance. A bidder has the power to withdraw his offer at any time before acceptance by the auctioneer.

If the sale is with reserve (meaning the owner may refuse bids), the offeror is the owner and the offeree the bidder. If the auction is without reserve, however, once the sale has begun and a bid has been entered, the goods cannot be withdrawn. But the bidder still may withdraw his bid at any time before the auctioneer accepts.

Types of Offers

There are two basic types of offers. The first is called *unilateral*. A unilateral offer is one promising the offeror to do something in return for an act by the offeree. This type of offer can be shown by the following examples: "I will pay you five dollars if you shovel the snow from my sidewalk," or "I promise to pay you ten dollars if you drive my car to California." These offers contemplate acceptance by performing the acts requested.

The second type of offer is called *bilateral*. The bilateral offer is a promise in return for another promise. Note the following examples: "I promise to pay you twenty dollars if you promise to sell me your tennis racket," or "I promise to pay you ten dollars if you promise to sell me your old coat next Thursday," or "I promise to trade my car for your truck on March 1, if you promise to trade your truck for my car on that date." In the case of a bilateral offer, a promise is requested instead of an act.

In the usual unilateral situation, when the offeree completes performance, a contract is formed. There is some question as to how the offeree need perform before a contract is formed. (This is discussed in the next Chapter entitled "Acceptance.")

Mutual Assent

A basic requisite for a contract is the mutual assent and agreement of the parties. Mutual assent can be expressed through words, conduct, or any other means which show that the parties have reached accord on the contractual terms.

The process of creating mutual assent begins with the making of an offer. Obviously, without some form of preliminary agreement to the conditions that are proposed by one party, no agreement can be formed. The proposition must be communicated to the person or persons with whom the offeror wishes to enter a contract. The offeree must know the conditions the offeror proposes.

In order to have mutual assent in a contract, the party to whom the offer is made must respond faithfully to the conditions of the offer. He must agree to do exactly what the offeror has proposed. In other words, both parties must concur with all the essential terms before a contract is recognized by the law. Only the expressed intent, or outward manifestations, of the parties is relevant; the secret intent of the contract is immaterial. The law looks only at the contract's explicit terms, not at the parties' interests. A party cannot later rely on unexpressed intent to negate or alter a contract. He cannot claim that he made the contract as a bluff or joke, or that there were conditions which he thought were in the contract. The assent must be present and not contingent on a future agreement. That is, a contract cannot be made to make an agreement in the future.

A so-called "objective look" is directed at the outward manifestations of both parties in order to determine whether a valid contract has been entered into. The acceptance of the offer by the offeree must be found to have been communicated to the offeror.

An example will be helpful. John Tyler owned two cars, a Mercedes and a Volkswagen. Both were new. One weekend, John told his neighbor that he would sell his car to him for $1,500. John meant the Volkswagen, but the neighbor thought he was referring to the Mercedes. The neighbor accepted, and two days later John parked the Volkswagen in front of the neighbor's home, rang the doorbell and said, "Well, here it is." The neighbor said "What do you mean? I bought a Mercedes." John said, "No you didn't." To resolve the dispute, John went to his lawyer who told him that there was no contract because there was no mutual assent. The parties had not agreed on what was to be purchased.

Termination of the Offer

Generally an offer will not terminate until either a specifically stated time stipulated in the offer has passed or, if no time was stated, until the lapse of a reasonable amount of time. During the period before the offer terminates, the offeree has a continuing power to form a contract by accepting the outstanding offer. For example, if the offer contains a statement that the offeree may accept only within a thirty-six-hour period, any attempted acceptance after that period will not constitute an acceptance.

An offer may also be terminated in the following ways:

1. Rejection by the offeree.
2. Death of one of the parties or destruction of the subject matter of the contract.
3. Legal prohibition of the contract.
4. Express revocation of the offer by the offeror before the stated time or a reasonable amount of time has elapsed.

If an offer is terminated, it may not be accepted later without a renewal of the offer by the offeror.

Rejection by the Offeree

If the person receiving the offer initially rejects it, the offer is terminated. He cannot change his mind later and accept it, even if the time limit specified for acceptance has not elapsed. A rejection of the offer must be communicated to the offeror to take effect. Thus, if I send a letter rejecting your offer, but before the letter is delivered to you, I personally contact you and make an acceptance, a contract has been formed. The later receipt of the rejection does not have any effect on the formation of the contract. It was complete when the offer was accepted before notice of rejection was received.

An inquiry as to the nature of the offer, or a request for a clarification of the terms, or for a slight change in the offer does not constitute an acceptance. Nor are such inquiries considered counteroffers, which would terminate the existing offer. The offer is alive until it is accepted, rejected, or revoked.

Lapse of Time or the Happening of a Condition in the Offer Causing Termination

As already noted, if there is no time limit specified in the offer during which the offeree may accept, the offer lapses within a reasonable period of time. This reasonable period is determined by the circumstances of the offer. The subject matter of the proposed contract is the most important factor. For example, in the case of an offer of perishable foods for sale, (for example, eggs), a reasonable time period would be short—possibly a day or two; while were the offer for the sale of land, a reasonable period would be much longer—as long as several months. The shifting of the market price of a commodity may also change the period of reasonableness. If the price of the good fluctuates daily, the reasonable time period is short; whereas if the commodity is stable in price, the period of time would be longer.

If an offer is made with a condition, and the condition ceases to exist, becomes illegal, or cannot be performed, the offer cannot be fulfilled, and there will be no contract. The offer is then terminated, and any attempted acceptance will, at most, be considered a counteroffer. For example, if John makes an offer to sell his house to Bill on condition that he is able to purchase another house on the same street, Bill can accept John's offer only when the latter purchases another house on that street.

Death or Insanity of a Party or Destruction of the Subject Matter of the Contract

Generally the death or insanity of the offeror terminates an offer. If the offeror should die before offeree makes his acceptance, there obviously cannot be any assent to the contract or its terms. This rule, however, is subject to an exception when the offeree of a unilateral offer (one calling for an act rather than a promise) completes the requested act, but the offeror dies before the return performance is tendered. In this case, the estate of the offeror is liable.

Regarding the destruction of the subject matter, the following example will be helpful. If Mr. Nickerson offers to sell you his summer cottage on Cape Cod, but prior to your acceptance, the house is destroyed by fire, your power to accept is void. The offer has terminated because of the destruction of the subject matter.

Legal Prohibition of the Contract

Any intervening action, conduct, or law which renders the proposed contract illegal terminates the offer. For example, you make an offer to Bill promising to sell him a certain amount of gold. Before Bill accepts, Congress passes a law forbidding the possession of gold by private individuals. The offer automatically terminates; an illegal contract will not be enforced by the courts.

Revocation of the Offer by the Offeror

Generally, the offeror can revoke his offer at any time before the offeree's acceptance. Once the offeree acquires knowledge of the revocation, he no longer can make an acceptance. Revocation can be made at any time, even though the offeror has promised not to revoke his offer. The only case in which the offeror may *not* revoke an offer occurs when the promise not to do so is accompanied by a payment of value by the offeree in return for the promise not to revoke. An example of this exception would be as follows: Bill gives Harry an option on land to purchase Blackacre for $6,000, irrevocable for three months. Harry pays Bill $20 for the option. Bill may then accept the offer (option) at any time within three months, and Harry may not revoke his offer for the stipulated period of time.

The intention and desire of the offeror to revoke the offer must be communicated to the offeree prior to an acceptance.

If the offeree should make an acceptance before learning of the revocation, a valid contract has been formed. The intended revocation is ineffective when received by the offeree. For example, suppose you offer to sell your house to your cousin Tom, but before Tom accepts you drop a revocation in the mail; an hour later you receive Tom's acceptance by telegram. As long as your letter of revocation did not reach Tom before he sent his acceptance, a valid contract has been formed.

But if the offeree has acquired knowledge, through any reliable source, that the offeror has revoked his offer, the offeree cannot later make an acceptance, and the offer is terminated. The only question at issue in this situation is the trustworthiness and validity of the source of information, which must be reasonably reliable.

If an offer is to a group or a certain class of people by a

particular method, such as a newspaper advertisement, revocation usually must be made in that same manner. If it was originally made in a newspaper advertisement, the revocation cannot be made over the radio or on television; it must be made through another newspaper advertisement. The reason for this rule is simple: only through the same method will the intended offerees learn of the revocation; a revocation by another method will, in most cases, be directed to another group.

If the offer calls for the offeree to perform a certain act (a unilateral contract), and the offeree begins the specified performance, there are three views as to whether there can be a revocation. The older, and now minority, view is that the offeror could revoke his offer at any time before the offeree's completed performance of the requested act, even though the offeror knows that the offeree has begun performance. Thus, in a contract to dig a ditch, the offer could be revoked up until the time the last shovelful of dirt was taken out.

The new, and now majority, view takes a more progressive approach and lessens some of the hardship which is cast upon the offeree under the older regulation. The new rule states that when an offeree of a unilateral contract has begun performance in reliance upon an offer, the offer has become irrevocable. The irrevocability takes effect once the offeree has begun performance.

A third view is that the offeror may revoke but he must pay the offeree for any work already done. For example, Mr. Clark offered Tom $10 to shovel the snow. Under the older rule, at any time before Tom completed shoveling the snow, Mr. Clark could revoke his offer and Tom would receive nothing. Under the new rule Mr. Clark cannot revoke his offer once Tom has begun performance. The third rule says that the offer may be revoked, but Tom must be paid at a reasonable rate for what he has done up to the revocation.

Counteroffers

A counteroffer is a proposal by the offeree, the person receiving the original offer. For example, if Farmer Jones offers to sell to a merchant ten bushels of apples for one dollar a bushel, and the merchant responds by saying that he will take eight bushels at ninety cents a bushel, the middleman's response amounts to a counteroffer. The counteroffer is not an acceptance, but is deemed another offer which the original offeror in turn may accept.

When Farmer Jones, in this illustration, tells the merchant that he accepts the proposal of eight bushels at ninety cents each, then a valid contract is formed. The counteroffer acts as a rejection of the original offer.

The counteroffer must be distinguished from negotiation or inquiry. If the merchant had said to Farmer Jones that he would like to buy the apples if Farmer Jones would lower his price, or that he would like to discuss other terms, the offer would still remain open, because the middleman's response was merely an inquiry. It does not act as a counterproposal, but only indicates the merchant's desire to pursue negotiations. A mere inquiry by the offeree regarding the offeror's willingness to change the terms of the offer, or his willingness to negotiate any terms, will not be considered a counteroffer and, thus, will not be a rejection either.

Acceptance upon certain conditions, e.g., that the offeror do something additional, will not act as an acceptance but rather as a counteroffer. For instance, in the last illustration, had the merchant stated that he would take Farmer's Jones' ten bushels of apples at one dollar per bushel if Jones would give him a free bushel of oranges, this statement would be viewed as a counteroffer.

Under the Uniform Commercial Code, Section 2-207, which applies to sales contracts between two or more parties, one of whom is a merchant, additional terms in an acceptance do not act as a counteroffer, unless the acceptance is made conditional upon the terms of the offer. These additional terms become part of the contract (between merchants), unless the offer expressly limits acceptance to the terms of the offer; or they materially alter it; or notification of objection to them has already been given, or is given within a reasonable time after notice of them is received.

4. Requirements for a Valid Contract Acceptance

OFFER AND acceptance are essential to the idea of a bargain between two parties, each receiving what he considers equivalent value to what he has given. Accepting an offer signals to the court that a bargain has been made; the offeree and offeror mutually assent to the terms of contract. The preceding Chapter considered the first step that had to be taken before formation of a contract—the offer. Here we treat the second step, the acceptance of the offer.

Acceptance Conforming to the Offer

An acceptance must conform to the conditions and requests of the offer. The person receiving the offer may not change terms or conditions which are contained in the offer. If he does, the reply is not an acceptance. If, however, additional terms, such as delivery, manner and place of shipment, are added by the offeree, they usually do not negate the accepted contract. Unless they are of the very essence of the offer, such as subject matter or price, they remain at the offeror's option to accept. Nevertheless, the new terms do not become part of the contract unless they are explicitly approved by the offeror.

The general rule is best stated by the Uniform Commercial

Code which allows the additional terms to form part of an effective acceptance so long as the offer does not make acceptance expressly conditional upon the exact terms of the offer, or if the terms of the acceptance do not materially alter the offer; *and* if objection to these terms is not given within a reasonable time after notice of the variant acceptance has been received. The code goes on to say that if the performance of the parties is sufficient to establish a contract, even though the writing is not, a contract will exist. The reason for this provision is to allow minor suggestions or proposals made by the offeree in his acceptance to be incorporated in the agreement without voiding the contract. These nonessential terms are mainly those that affect the time, place, and manner of delivery. An example of this is when the offeree, in his acceptance, adds that he will take delivery on the first of next month. Surely this statement should not negate the contract. Under the common law the rule was that *any* additions would negate an acceptance. If the offer stated that payment was to be in the form of a mailed money order and the acceptance noted, "I'll bring the cash over," no valid acceptance had taken place, and no contract was formed.

It can be inferred from the offeree's acceptance, if it is not made in the exact language of the offer but is a mere "yes," or "I accept," that he agrees to all of the terms contained in the offer.

Timing of Acceptance

Logically enough, the acceptance must come after the offer. Even where an offer calls for a certain performance, if performance is rendered prior to making an offer or without knowledge of an existing offer, the offeree cannot claim that there was an acceptance. For example: John returns Mrs. Clark's lost dog without any knowledge that a reward is being offered. Therefore, John cannot claim to have made an acceptance because he never had knowledge of the outstanding offer. Thus, without knowledge of an outstanding offer, it is impossible to have an acceptance or a contract.

The acceptance becomes part of the agreement in which the offeror agrees to the terms contained in the offer. There is conflicting opinion as to whether an offeree has validly accepted an offer in those instances where he has begun performance prior to learning about the offer, and completes performance hoping to accept the offer. Under the modern view, the offeree has entered into a valid contract even though he has partially performed prior to acquiring knowledge of an outstanding offer.

The offeree, upon making acceptance, is saying two things: first, he is giving the offeror his requested return in replying to the offer; and second, he is assenting to the proposed contract by agreeing to all the terms contained therein.

Notification of Acceptance

The acceptance should be in the same form as the offer. More important, however, is that the intention of the offeree to agree to enter into the proposed contract be communicated to the offeror. This notification to the offeror is dispensable only in some situations where the offer is a request for an act or for forbearance of an act. One such instance is a unilateral contract.

For example, Mr. Clark offers to pay Billy five dollars to shovel the snow from his sidewalk. Billy begins the job without notifying Mr. Clark, who can easily observe the boy from his window. Billy need not notify Mr. Clark that he has begun because the offeror had a reasonable opportunity to acquire this knowledge. Billy did not have to give notice prior to performance. Commencing the performance constituted an acceptance. If, however, Mr. Clark had had no chance to observe Billy at work—and it may be inferred from the circumstances that Mr. Clark wished to know—Billy's notification to Mr. Clark prior to performance may be necessary to form a valid acceptance.

Who May Accept an Offer

Acceptance can be made only by a person to whom the offer is directed. Except under certain circumstances mentioned later, the offeree cannot delegate his power of acceptance to another. Only the party or parties named in the offer have the power to make an acceptance. If Ed offers to sell his automobile to John for $500, John's brother cannot accept Ed's offer. Any attempt made by John's brother to accept the offer can only be treated as an offer for the purchase of the automobile, which Ed must in turn accept to form a valid contract.

If an offer is made to the entire nation (as in an advertisement), anyone may accept. On the other hand, if it is only made to a specific group of people whose united performance is needed to complete the contract, the entire group must make the acceptance. If it is made to any member of that group, any one of them may accept. The requirement of mutual assent to a contract is fulfilled only if the offer is accepted by the party to whom it is addressed; once a contract is created, however, duties and rights under that contract may in certain cases involve or benefit third parties.

Communication of Acceptance by Correspondence

We have seen that it is necessary to communicate acceptance to the offeror, especially where the offer calls for a promise rather than an act of forbearance on the part of the offeree. For example, the offeror, A, requests that the offeree, B, make a return promise to him. The contract is not complete until this return promise is communicated to the offeror. Two theories explain when acceptance is valid if communication is made by mail: the first says the offer is accepted when the letter is posted; the second says acceptance is not valid until receipt of the letter by the offeror. Most states agree with the former rule—although a substantial number of western states follow the latter regulation.

The communication of an acceptance leads to problems if the offeror decides to revoke his offer. The difficulty arises in deciding whether there was a valid acceptance prior to revocation. The various states resolve this problem in any one of four different ways:

1. The acceptance and the revocation are both valid on dispatch—that is, at the time of mailing—and this is determined by the post mark.

2. The acceptance and the revocation are complete on receipt, and the one received first is effective.

3. Acceptance is complete on dispatch; revocation is complete upon receipt.

4. Acceptance is complete on receipt; revocation is complete on dispatch.

The majority of jurisdictions use rule No. 3. When the acceptance is sent, the contract is formed. If there is a revocation by the offeror, notice to that effect must reach the offeree before he posts his acceptance in order for the offer to be revoked. If I send out a letter offering to sell my horse for ten dollars and the next day I call you to revoke the offer, but one hour before the call you have mailed me an acceptance, the revocation is not good and a contract has been formed.

The type of communication required for the acceptance must usually be the same as that used in the offer. If an offer is sent by mail, it is implied that an acceptance also be sent through the mail. The same rule applies to telephone and telegraph. The older view was that if an offer was received by a certain method of communication, such as the telegraph, the only valid method of acceptance would be by telegram. A telephone call or a letter would be null and void. Previously this rule was strictly applied. In recent years most courts have liberalized this view, holding that if an offer is sent through the mail, acceptance may be made via telephone or telegram. The modern rule is to allow any reasonable method of acceptance that, depending on the circumstances, is considered reasonable. The offeree is safe, however, if he accepts by the same means in which the offer was communicated; on the other hand, if the offer specifies a certain method of communication, the offeree must communicate his acceptance in the requested manner to form a valid contract.

Silence as an Acceptance

In certain instances, silence can act as an acceptance. One situation exists where the offeror specifically states in his offer that silence is to be considered as acceptance. However, courts are understandably wary of imposing a duty upon the offeree who has disregarded an offer which stipulates that silence constitutes acceptance. Otherwise, lost and destroyed mail, as well as the acts of unscrupulous individuals, would give rise to a multitude of unjust and unapproved contracts.

The second circumstance under which silence may act as acceptance would be a case in which the offeror presumes from the offeree's silence that there has been a valid acceptance. Thus, an insurance company will send to the insured an offer to renew an already-existing household insurance policy. If the renewal offer is not returned with some notice of cancellation, it is presumed that the insured's silence constitutes an acceptance. Today most courts adopt this view. The contrary position, that an acceptance cannot be implied until the company receives payment of the premiums, is the older view.

The modern view is that when the insured has had a reasonable time to reject the policy, but instead he accepts benefits from it, an acceptance is deemed to have been made. Evidence that the parties have had previous dealings will tend to create an acceptance when the offeree remains silent.

This is to be distinguished from situations in which unsolicited material is sent with a notice that it must be accepted or returned within 30 days. Christmas cards and other material from religious organizations are classic examples. The receiver of such goods is, in almost all states, not obliged to do anything with this type of material. The law does not allow someone to force a contract on a person.

The states themselves have attempted to regulate the flow of unsolicited materials to unwary recipients by means of stringent legislation. Typical of this type of legislation is the recent Massachusetts law (MGLA c. 275 543; approved May 8, 1969) which clarifies the responsibility for unsolicited goods in this manner:

> Any person who receives unsolicited goods, wares, or merchandise, offered for sale, but not actually ordered or requested by him orally or in writing, shall be entitled to consider such goods, wares, or merchandise an unconditional gift, and he may use or dispose of the same as he sees fit without obligation on his part to the sender.

Conditional Acceptance

If the offeree, in his purported acceptance, states a condition upon which he will accept the offer, no contract has been formed. This type of acceptance will generally act as a counter-offer. If a farmer offers to sell to a dealer 300 bushels of grain at two dollars a bushel, and the dealer replies that he will accept the offer if the farmer will pay delivery costs, the dealer's reply constitutes a conditional acceptance, which is, in reality, a rejection of the offer, and at best may be considered a counteroffer. If the farmer agrees to the dealer's delivery terms, a contract will be formed. The dealer's reply acts as a counteroffer and not as an acceptance, because the differing terms lack mutual assent.

Certain conditions that may be included in the acceptance will not make the acceptance a counteroffer. These conditions are usually implied in the offer. For instance, this type of condition occurs when the seller offers a certain piece of land and the buyer, in making his acceptance, adds that he will accept only if the seller conveys *good title* (ownership unencumbered by liens or mortgages). Since good title is usually an implied term in any contract for the sale of land, the addition of this condition will have no adverse effect on the formation of the contract. However, if the seller states that he will give a *quitclaim deed,* (which means that the buyer takes only such interest in the property as the seller can convey), then the buyer's additional stipulation—that he will accept only good title—will not act as an acceptance, but merely as a counteroffer.

Certain other conditions which may be stated in the acceptance without acting as a rejection or as a counteroffer are those which are a matter of custom and trade usage. For example, if the dealer responds to an offer for the sale of 100 bushels of grain, but adds that he will not accept the 100 bushels unless they are shipped in the particular type of bushel baskets customarily used by the trade, the reply will create an acceptance and not a counteroffer. Because it is the custom in the trade, the use of this type of basket is considered implied in the contract.

5. Requirements for a Valid Contract Consideration

General

IN ADDITION to a valid offer and acceptance, another element is necessary to the formation of a contract—*consideration.* Consideration is something of value that changes hands between the parties to the contract. Each must render legally adequate consideration to the other in order to form a contract. Without giving consideration, which the law views as valuable, a party is merely the intended recipient of a gift, and the other's performance is unenforceable. Thus, a contract cannot exist without consideration which may be the exchange of any of the following:

1. a promise for a promise;
2. forbearance for a promise;
3. an act for a promise; or
4. the mutual establishment, modification, change, or destruction of a legal relationship; or
5. such a modification or change for a promise.

Consideration must be agreed upon in the contractual exchange, and this bargained-for consideration must be sufficient or "valuable" in the eyes of the law. Without the sufficiency of consideration there will be no contract. In a bilateral contract, consideration is the return promise; in a unilateral contract the consideration is an act or forbearance from an act.

Consideration is a rather difficult concept to define; however a few examples should help to illustrate what is and what is not sufficient consideration.

1. *A promise for a promise:* If I promise to sell you my car for $500, and you promise to buy it for that amount, the mutual promises are sufficient consideration.

2. *Forbearance for a promise:* I promise you $100 if you refrain from leaving the state for one week. Your forbearance to move from the state will act as sufficient consideration in return for my valuable consideration of $100 to complete the contract.

3. *An act for a promise:* If I promise you ten dollars to shovel the snow from my walk, and you complete the work, this act will be sufficient consideration for a contract.

4. *Any establishment, modification, change, or destruction of legal relationship:* If you and I have a contract whereby you are to deliver a gallon of milk each day for monthly payment, and during the existence of this contract we agree to new terms—for example, one half gallon a day instead of a gallon—we destroy the old contract and incorporate the revised terms into a new contract. The destruction of the old contractual relationship in order to create a new one will act as sufficient consideration.

Consideration, then, is that thing gained or lost in a contract. Sometimes it may not appear to be very material—as in example No. 2—but as long as it is present, the contract is valid.

Sufficiency of Consideration

In order for a promise to be made binding upon the party, there must be some consideration in return from the party to whom the benefits of the promise attach. If no return consideration accompanies a promise, it is merely a gift, and the promisor is not liable if he refuses to make the gift because no return consideration was attached to the promise of a gift. Therefore, if Charlie promises his nephew, Peter, a watch for his birthday but later fails to give him the gift, no court would compel Charlie to buy Peter the watch. However if Charlie promises to give Peter a new watch if Peter stops smoking for a month, and Peter keeps that promise, almost any court would order the uncle to buy the watch for his nephew. The difference between the two situations is that, in the latter instance, Peter has given up something, and this forbearance constitutes a sufficient consideration (although the value to Charlie probably resides solely in eliminating worry about the boy's health). The consideration for the promise is that which is exchanged, or given, for the return promise.

In order for consideration to be sufficient, it must usually constitute a benefit to the promisor or a detriment to the promisee. One may exist without the other, although they are usually found together. Thus, the cash payment of $20 for the delivery of a hat constitutes a detriment to the promisee (who spends $20) and a benefit to the promisor (who receives the money in return for delivery of the hat). Detriment ordinarily qualifies as consideration in most cases, no matter how slight. The promisee may only be asked to walk across the street in return for something highly valuable; if he does so, an enforceable contract exists. In most cases, the law is concerned only with whether or not there *is* detriment, not with how much. But the benefit or detriment must be what has been bargained for.

The Concept of Bargain

In order for consideration to be legally sufficient, it must be bargained for between the parties. If there is no bargain for value given, no consideration exists and hence, no contract. If one promises to perform an act, and the one to whom the promise is made has not bargained for or requested its performance, the promise is not enforceable. Moreover, if the promised performance is rendered, the law will not require payment for its execution (except in unusual circumstances) because in order for detriment to be validly bargained for, it must occur *after* the promise was made. That is, if Peter had refrained from smoking *prior* to his uncle's offer of a new watch, there would not have been a valid bargain at that time because the promise was made after the forbearance.

Pre-existing Legal Obligations

If I owe you a valid debt of $100, and you agree to accept $75 as payment in full, you can later enforce payment of the other $25. The reason given by the courts is that there is no consideration for reducing the debt's amount. If I promise to pay $75 on the same conditions as the $100, this cannot be called consideration since I am already under a legal obligation to pay you the entire $100. However, if I suffer some form of detriment in the new promise—such as agreeing to make the smaller payment at an earlier date—legally sufficient consideration exists in the change in payment terms, and a new contract is formed.

Therefore, when a contracted debt is reduced to a lesser sum, with some added detriment to the debtor, or where the form of the debt is materially changed, detriment constituting valuable consideration has been incurred by the debtor, and a new contractual relationship is established. For example, if in lieu of paying a debt, a debtor agrees with his creditor that he will not enter into a particular business within a certain area for five years, forbearance of competition with the creditor by the debtor would be sufficient consideration for the release from indebtedness. The mere fact that the detriment suffered cannot be measured in dollars makes no difference.

If the promisor intends to make a gift, no detriment will occur by his performance. For example, if I tell you that when you come to my house, I will give you my old lawn mower, it is a gift if I so intended. Your trip to my house will not constitute sufficient detriment to act as consideration, because I did not bargain for it. But if my intention was conditional upon the performance of your coming to my house, then there would be sufficient detriment.

In some instances, the promise of a gift may be enforceable. When "artificial" consideration has been promised, a valid contract is occasionally found to exist. An example of "artificial" consideration is the term "one dollar and other valuable consideration," used often in options for the sale of land. Although no money actually changes hands, the law interprets this statement to mean that the parties have sufficiently bargained for the agreement, and the requisite detriment and benefit have occurred. Some courts thus hold that the payment of one dollar is not necessary when the statement is contained in a written option contract. The mere mention of the statement is sufficient to create legal consideration.

Adequacy of Consideration

Normally the law will not take into account the *adequacy* of the consideration (meaning the amount or value of the consideration given or received). The court will not declare a contract void for lack of consideration even if its terms were $20 for the Hope Diamond. The law does not look into the adequacy of what is exchanged, except in certain situations that will be discussed later. The law will not look into how fair a bargain is, but only if a bargain exists. If the bargain and agreement were initially made to the satisfaction of both parties, without fraud, duress, or undue influence, the law will not question the parties' judgment regarding the fairness of the transaction.

If I should agree to exchange my three-year-old car for your new one, and there was no fraud or illegality involved, I cannot claim later that the bargain was unfair. The law will consider irrelevant the respective values of the old and the new cars. If I have an option to buy your land and have given you "one dollar and other valuable consideration" (a standard formal statement in option-contracts) to hold the option open for one month, even though the land is worth far more than one dollar, the law will consider the stated sum sufficient to keep the option open.

When the bargained-for act creates neither benefit nor detriment to the parties, it is insufficient, inadequate and unenforceable by the court. If I agree to give up my right to collect a debt from you, but the debt was barred from collection because it was illegally incurred—for example, a gambling debt—the agreement becomes entirely void because of inadequate and insufficient consideration. No benefit could arise by my giving up the right to collect, because the debt was not legally collectable, and no detriment could occur because the holder of the note was not giving up anything.

However, if the note had some value—no matter how remote the possibility of collection was—there would be sufficient detriment and benefit for the courts to consider the giving up of the note adequate.

Forbearance as Consideration

Generally, the forbearance of an act, a power, a privilege, or any legal action by the promisee will constitute valid and binding consideration. For example, if Peter promises his uncle to give up drinking for six months, Peter's forbearance from liquor will be good consideration. This would be so even if Peter were below the legal drinking age. If I gave up the right to bring a valid lawsuit, this forbearance would act as sufficient consideration—even if I were likely to lose the suit. However, I must have had some valid claim upon which to bring a cause of action. A frivolous claim will not act as sufficient consideration, nor will the possibility of a claim which might arise in the future. If my promise was to refrain from suing under a contract which never existed or one that might arise at some future date, neither promise would constitute sufficient consideration.

If I agree to refrain from some action in which I have a legal right to engage, this forbearance acts as a detriment and is sufficient consideration. Even if I never seriously considered engaging in the act, as long as it is legal, relinquishing my right to perform this action is sufficient consideration.

A Pre-existing Duty as Consideration

Normally, a bargained-for promise is good consideration. An exemption to this rule is created when the promised performance is already owed to the promise. That is, when a person is bound by a previous contract to execute an act, a new promise to perform the already existing obligation will not create consideration for a new bargain. If I have made a contract with the city of New York to plow snow from certain streets at a fixed price, I cannot later bargain for another contract to plow these same streets at a higher price. Since I am legally obligated under the contract to plow these streets, any further bargaining on the same subject on identical terms has no value to the city. However, the pre-existing duty must be contained in a legally binding agreement. If the obligation were not enforceable, offering identical terms of a void contract for a new one at a higher price is sufficient consideration for the validation of a new contract.

However, if the original contract is unenforceable, a new agreement may be formed by the parties on exactly the same terms, and those terms will constitute valid consideration. If I had entered into a contract with you to perform certain services for an agreed price, but due to fraud the fact that the contract should have been in writing and was in oral form, a new contract that involved no fraud—or had been put in writing—would be valid, the old terms serving as sufficient consideration.

In some states, an exception is allowed in the case of building contracts. If a builder finds that he cannot do the job at the agreed on contract price, his rebargaining the pre-existing constitution duty at a higher price will not make the contract invalid. The reasoning is rather easy to see: courts have considered it in society's interest to allow contractors to renegotiate rather than to breach a contract and leave the work half-done. The situation often arises in which the actual costs of completing a structure prohibitively exceed the costs set forth in a contract signed months or even years before actual construction begins. By then the price of concrete, bricks, and other materials has risen so much that the builder may prefer to break the contract, and take his chances in court rather than risk bankruptcy by performing. This exception does not mean that the builder can change the terms of a contract at will, but merely that if they are changed by a new agreement and the builder sues for payment of the higher price, the other party cannot use the defense of a pre-existing obligation.

Consideration in the Bi-lateral Contract

The bilateral contract, then, is composed of a promise made by one party in return for a promise from another party. The exchanged promises constitute a valid contract if they were bargained for by the parties and if a legally enforceable detriment or benefit arises from each promise which did not exist prior to the formation of the contract. The mutual promises act as consideration. Thus, if I promise to pay you five dollars and you promise to sell me your gold watch, our mutual promises are sufficient consideration to establish a binding contract.

Along with these mutual promises, there must be mutual obligation (called by the courts, *mutuality of promise* and *mutuality of obligation* respectively). That is, each promise must legally bind the party giving it. If I have made a promise to you from which I have the ability to withdraw at any time, I have not bound myself to do anything, and the contract is not enforceable.

Substitutes for Consideration

There are some situations in which a valid contract is formed although consideration would not seem to be present. In a limited number of cases, courts have allowed something to substitute for valid consideration.

Reliance

If you have reasonably relied on a gratuitous pledge—thinking that the promised performance is legally enforceable—and in the process you have suffered detriment, the promise is enforceable in some states, even though no bargained-for consideration exists. You are said to have relied upon the promise.

For example, Mrs. Peters promises her niece an automobile if she agrees to take care of her for two years. Without actually promising to care for her aunt, the niece nevertheless does so for two years. Although there is no bargained-for consideration given by the niece—that is, Mrs. Peters asked for a promise, not performance—all courts would award the niece the price of an automobile because she relied upon her aunt's promise to her detriment.

Pledges

Assume that I have pledged $100,000 to the Heart Fund, and the Fund has procured my promise in good faith. Relying upon my pledge to donate, the Heart Fund signs a contract to construct a research center; however, I make no attempt to void my pledge. Under these circumstances, the law could enforce my contribution. On the other hand, had the Fund taken no reliance action upon my pledge, most courts would hold that the grounds were insufficient to enforce my contribution.

The requirement of bargain contracts is somewhat lessened in the case of an individual's making a subscription to charity. Normally a person's pledge would be merely an unenforceable promise to make a gift at some future date. However, in order to protect charitable institutions against the withdrawal of subscriptions, the courts have applied the reliance reasoning.

Contracts under Seal

At common law, any contract containing a seal was binding on the parties, even though the agreement lacked consideration.

If I promised you a horse for your birthday, the promise was (and is) not enforceable because it lacks consideration. It is a gift.

However, if I had sealed the written instrument which contained the promise, I would have been bound to make the gift to you. The seal was a substitute for a consideration. Had the agreement been made under seal, nothing else would have been necessary. Although the importance of the seal has declined considerably, in some states it is still used in contract situations where consideration is lacking. An example would be a case in which the parties, who already have an unsealed contract, agree to a lesser sum of money due on the contract, thus forming a new contract. Ordinarily this new agreement would not be binding, since no new consideration exists for the reduction of the debt; however, if a seal is added by the debtor, some courts will enforce the new contract.

The seal makes what would be considered an unenforceable gift in the amount of the reduction, an enforceable contract. Putting the agreement under seal changes the old relationship and binds the parties in a validly enforceable contract.

A seal cannot make an illegal contract valid; for example, neither sealed nor unsealed gambling contracts are enforceable where gambling is illegal. This rule applies to any contract which would not be binding, even if good consideration were attached.

Any new contract supported by adequate consideration can modify or rescind the original sealed instrument. There does not have to be—as under common law—another sealed instrument revoking the original contract.

In approximately thirty states, the seal is not a substitute for consideration. Six other states have adopted a modified form of the old common law rule.

6. Requirements for a Valid Contract Form and Certainty

IF THE average person is asked whether a contract must be in writing to be enforceable, he will usually answer yes. However, for the most part, his reply would be wrong. It is a general principle of our law that all agreements are enforceable, whether they are in writing or not. Only in a limited number of circumstances must a contract be in written form to take on validity.

The Statute of Frauds is a law which makes written contracts mandatory in certain situations. Every jurisdiction has some version of the Statute of Frauds, and although they differ from state to state, these statutes are usually very similar because they have all descended from the original English Statute of Frauds, passed in 1677. When America was settled, the colonial legislatures enacted versions of this statute modeled closely on the parent English statute. After independence, the statutes became state laws, the newer states copying theirs from the older ones. The first part of this section will be an examination of which kinds of contracts are required by the majority of American state laws to be in writing. We will accomplish this by examining the provisions of a typical Statute of Frauds, describing some significant variations as we proceed.

When Writing is Necessary (The Statute of Frauds)

The most logical place to start is with the British statute, upon which most American laws are closely patterned. Usually courts do not like to apply the Statute of Frauds; they generally desire to enforce a contractual promise, even if the parties have not had the foresight to put their bargain into writing. The interpretation of the Statute of Frauds is complicated, because of the many attempts by courts to avoid the statute's strict requirements in the interests of justice in individual cases. Very often the words of the Statute of Frauds carry a good deal less force than they seem to.

The original Statute of Frauds contained twenty-five sections and provisions. Many of these provisions are irrelevant today since basically they are concerned with ancient property law. Two sections, however, still have great influence in the field of contract law. The first states that, unless in writing, no action shall be brought to enforce the following:

1. Contracts in which one person promises to pay the debts of another.

2. Promises made in exchange for a promise of marriage.

3. Contracts for the sale of land or for the sale of any interest in land.

4. Contracts which require more than one year to perform.

The second relevant part of the statute provides that no contract for the sale of goods in excess of a given value shall be enforced unless:

1. the buyer has accepted part of the goods; or,

2. the buyer has paid part of the purchase price; or,

3. some note or written memorandum was made of the agreement and was signed by the party to be charged; that is, the party against whom the court is asked to enforce the contract.

The purpose of the statute is to prevent fraud and perjury in the making of contracts. Obviously, when contracts are not in writing, it is much easier for dishonest men to change the terms by lying. Thus, the requirement of writing reduces controversy. Even where no fraud or dishonesty is present, this regulation is often useful; where, for example, both sides have forgotten what the exact terms of the original agreement were. (This latter reason indicates why contracts which take more than a year to perform were included under the statute.)

A second aim of the statute is to deter people from entering into important contracts too hastily. If the parties who are making the contract have to write down the terms of their agreement, they are more likely to consider carefully what they are doing. This prevents them from making rash and impulsive bargains. The inclusion of marriage contracts and binding agreements to pay another's debts can be explained on these grounds as well.

Generally speaking, the types of contracts included in the statute are those which, in 1677, were the most complex or important of the agreements that people commonly made. Of course, changes in our economic and political system have produced a situation in which some of the most significant and involved agreements are not covered by the Statute of Frauds. In America, the individual states have filled these gaps by amending the original statute. A New York statute, for example, requires that arbitration agreements be in writing.

Now, we shall consider separately each type of contract included in the statute and give a general idea of what each one means.

Promises to Pay the Debt of Another

The statute requires that such promises be in writing; however, the promise need not be to pay exactly the same thing that the debtor owes. As long as the payment pledged is accepted in satisfaction of another's debt, the commitment must be in writing to be enforceable against the person promising payment. For example, suppose you owe Fred $250 and you have given him an I.O.U. for that amount, whereupon I promise to give Fred my stereo set if he will destroy your I.O.U., thus settling the debt. If Fred accepts the promise of a stereo set as a discharge of your debt to him, then my promise must be in writing. It makes no difference that the debt is $250 and the promised payment is a stereo set.

If a promise has as its *leading object* the payment of another's debt, it must be in writing. If, however, the main reason for making the promise has a different objective, and erasing your debt is merely a secondary consequence, then the promise need not be in writing. For example, my promise of a stereo set might be intended primarily as a gift to induce Fred to deal directly with me in connection with some business negotiation. Although I have satisfied your debt to him, this promise need not be in writing, unless it falls within another section of the Statute of Frauds. In such a case, the payment of your debt is only secondary to my own self-interest in a business transaction.

The promise need not be to pay all of another's debt. Thus, if you owe Joe $100, and I promise to pay him $50, the promise still must be in writing, even though your obligation is not completely satisfied.

The promise must be a direct answer for another's debt, not one which substitutes a new obligation. For example, suppose you owe Fred $100 and I promise him to pay your debt. If the promise is worded in those terms, it must be written. If my promise is that I will pay Fred if you don't, it must also be written. Your debt to Fred still exists after a promise of this nature; the only difference is that I have guaranteed the repayment of your indebtedness.

On the other hand, if I promise to pay Fred $100 to eradicate your debt, Fred's acceptance would necessitate the drawing up of a new contract in which *I* would owe him $100, and, unlike the previous situation, you would owe him nothing. In this case, the promise is not covered by the Statute of Frauds and, therefore, need not be in writing. The reason is that the Statute of Frauds states that promises to *answer for* the debt of another must be in writing. In the second example, I have not answered for your debt; instead, I have made a new contract with your creditor, thus assuming the debt myself which I must pay Fred.

The debt need not be a financial obligation. It can be any sort of legal duty that one person owes to another. For example, if you make a contract with Fred to wash dishes, your duty to perform that chore is considered a debt by the Statute of Frauds. Therefore, if I guarantee your performance, if and when you fail to do so, my promise would have to be in writing to be enforceable.

Finally, the promise must be made to the one to whom the debt is owed. For example, suppose that you owe Fred $100. If I promise *Fred* that I will pay him if he cannot collect from you, that commitment must be in writing. But if I promise *you* that I will pay Fred for you, my promise need not be in writing. The promise must be made to the creditor for the Statute of Frauds to apply.

Interests in Land

The section of the Statute of Frauds which deals with interests in land was the most important one. It states that "no action shall be brought . . . upon any contract or sale of lands, tenements or hereditaments, or any interest concerning them, unless that contract is in writing."

Although important, the section has a rather limited application in modern society because contract law is not ordinarily central to real estate transactions. Real estate is subject to property law which has a separate and different set of rules.

Contract law is important to land transfers in those cases where the parties make a contract to exchange or sell land at some future time. (This is often called an *option contract* or simply an *option*.) They usually precede formal transfers of property or deeds. Contract law and the Statute of Frauds are applicable to these contracts.

The *tenements* and *hereditaments* mentioned in the statute refer to buildings which, by custom, have been considered part of a tract of land, and to personal possessions which passes along with the property to heirs. The use of these terms is rare in modern times, and many state statutes do not include the words "tenements" or "hereditaments."

The "contract of sale" mentioned in the Statute of Frauds need not be a sale for money. If the contract involves a mutual exchange of land or an exchange of goods for land, the contract must be in writing.

The most complicated part of this section of the statute is that which requires the sale of "any interest" in land be in writing. Courts have had difficulty in deciding exactly what is and what is not an interest in land. It may be less than complete ownership with several people having an interest in the same piece of land. For example, I may own land and can transfer to you the oil rights beneath it.

The courts have decided that the following constitute an interest in land, which cannot be sold or bought unless the contract is in writing:

1. *Life estates:* a life estate results when one transfers land to another for only as long as the recipient lives. Ownership then reverts to the original proprietor to a third person. The creation of a life estate is not valid unless in writing.

2. *Fee simple:* fee simple is complete ownership of a piece of land.

3. *Fee tail:* a complex hereditary interest in land which, though extremely rare, is still in existence.

4. *Leases:* Any lease of land which lasts for more than a year must be in writing to be enforceable.

5. *Remainders:* This is another technical hereditary interest in land. A remainder exists where, for example, a person dies and wills land to a second party for the length of his life, and

further provides that the land will go to a third party when the second party dies. The third party, therefore, has a remainder interest in the land, and to be valid, the remainder interest statement must be in writing.

6. *Trusts:* A trust exists where one person has the use and benefit of a piece of land, but another person owns legal title to it. For example, I own legal title to a piece of land, but you have the right to farm it and to receive all the produce it yields. Either you or I can contract to sell our separate interests in the land, but to do so validly, we must put the contract in writing.

7. *Mortgages and liens:* These are interests in land which must be in writing. A lien on real estate is very similar to a mortgage and gives the lien holder the right to sell the land and receive the proceeds of the sale if the owner fails to fulfill some obligation specified in the lien.

8. *Easements:* an easement is the right to do a specified thing on a piece of land owned by another. An example of an easement is the right of the telephone company to string wires over another man's land.

9. *Restrictive covenants:* a restrictive covenant exists when land is sold subject to some condition. Thus, if I sold you a piece of land with the provision that it could not be used for coal mining, a restrictive covenant on the use of the land would be in force. While some courts regard such a restriction as an interest in land, others feel that it is not. The majority view is that they are interests in land which must be in writing to be enforced by the courts.

10. *Assets connected to the land:* such assets as timber and buildings are construed to be an interest in land; crops are occasionally considered to be an interest in land. If I owned a cornfield and agreed to sell the yield to you, I would not be selling an interest in the land; therefore, the agreement need not be in writing. The question of whether the sale of trees on a piece of land must be in writing presents more of a problem. If the buyer gets ownership before the trees are cut, this is usually considered an interest. If the trees have already been

cut down, however, the timber is not usually considered an "interest." Other circumstances may help courts in making a decision; for instance, if the buyer and the seller considered the trees to be part of the land, there would be no question.

Promises Made in Exchange for a Promise of Marriage

Any promise made in exchange for a promise to marry must be in writing to be enforceable. This section of the Statute of Frauds can be explained by a series of examples: 1) John promises to give Marsha a yacht, if she will promise to marry him; this contract must be in writing. 2) John promises to give Marsha a yacht, but only *after* she has married him; this contract must also be in writing. In the first example, John promises to give the yacht in exchange for Marsha's *promise*. In the second example, John's promise is given in exchange for an *actual wedding ceremony*.

3) John and Marsha promise to marry each other. This legally phrased engagement constitutes a contract which, in the ordinary case, is simple to enforce whether in writing or not. However, should Marsha change her mind, John could not compel her to marry him; nor would the court award him damages for Marsha's *breach of promise of marriage*. If Marsha were spiteful or caused John monetary damage through her actions, John could sue in tort and recover. Courts have thus refused to apply the Statute of Frauds to engagements unless there is a property settlement in conjunction with the betrothal. Therefore, engagements need not be in writing, unless they involve promises of yachts, money, or other property.

Contracts which do not involve a *direct* transfer of property must also be in writing as they provide for the regulation of property rights between husband and wife. For example, if John and Marsha promise to marry each other, and also agree that their present ownership of property would not be affected by the marriage, the contract must be in writing.

The contract in consideration of marriage does not have to be between the two people contemplating marriage. It may be made by the parents of the couple or by two of their friends, relatives, or business associates, and must be in writing.

Contracts Requiring More Than One Year to Perform

This part of the Statute of Frauds has been construed narrowly by the courts which have restricted its application. The section applies, then, only where it is completely impossible for a contract to be performed within a year. As a result, many contracts which would seem to fall within this provision do not. An example of this will demonstrate how the "one year" clause of the statute is restricted.

I agree to build a house for you, and you promise to pay me $20,000 when it is finished. Both of us agree that the house must be completed in less than four years. It takes me three years to build the house. Even though I required much longer than one year to build the house, the contract need not be in writing, because it would have been physically possible and legally permissible for me to have built the house in *less* than one year. It makes no difference that both you and I thought when we made the contract, that it would take me much longer than a year. The fact that the contract deadline is four years hence—well in excess of one year—is also irrelevant.

However if a contract provides that some transaction be performed more than one year in the future, the agreement must be in writing, even though the actual performance may take less than a year. For example, suppose you and I make a contract in 1966, and we agree that in 1969 I will build a swimming pool for you. Although it will take me only one month to build the pool, the contract must be in writing, because the performance will take place more than a year in the future. It is impossible for me to complete the pool within a year because, under the contract, I cannot begin until 1969.

If, on the other hand, the contract provides that I will build a pool for you if you buy a house, the contract need not be in writing. This is so even though we make the contract in 1966, and you do not buy a house until 1969. It was possible, at the time the contract was made, that the transaction would be carried out within one year. Even if it is highly unlikely that you would buy a house in less than a year—or, for that matter, if it is most unlikely that you would ever buy a house—the contract need not be in writing. In fact, as long as there is the slightest possibility that the contract may be performed within a year it need not be in writing—unless, of course, it falls within another section of the statute.

Some contracts provide that one party render his services for an indefinite period of time. Such contracts need not be in writing if there is any chance at all that the indefinite duration of performance will end before one year is up. For example, we agree that I will mow your lawn until you die. It is possible that you will live for 50 years; however, since there is a chance that you will die before the end of the year, the contract need not be in writing.

Some contracts provide that one person shall serve another for a specified period of time. If the period agreed upon is less than one year, the contract need not be in writing; otherwise it must be. For example, I agree to mow your lawn for the next five years. This contract must be in writing, even though it is possible that you will die within the year and thereby terminate the contract. The reason is that the contract specifies a five year period, clearly intending that I work for more than one year. The previous example of mowing your lawn until you die does not intend for my performance to last for a specified period of time; therefore, it does not necessarily intend that I work for more than one year.

For the purpose of the Statute of Frauds, most states agree that a year is 365 days; fractions of a day are not counted. Therefore, if a contract provided for a job that would take 365½ days to do, the agreement would not have to be in writing.

Some agreements provide for a job that will take more than a year to do, but add that the contract can be cancelled by either of the parties involved. Such contracts usually do not have to be in writing. For example, suppose you and I agree that I will shovel your walk for five years, and we also agree that either of us can cancel the agreement by giving two weeks' notice. Such a contract usually does not have to be in writing, because there is a possibility of termination in less than a year.

Some contracts have provisions which one party can perform within a year, whereas the other party needs more than a year to carry out his side of the bargain. Such contracts must be in writing, because the contract as a whole will not be finished within one year. For example, if I promise to build a swimming pool in exchange for your promise to clear my driveway of snow for five years, the contract must be in writing. I can build the pool in less than a year, but it will take you five years to fulfill your obligation.

Sale of Goods

The final provision of the original Statute of Frauds which we will examine requires that certain contracts for the sale of goods be in writing, unless the value of the merchandise sold was less than $100 in most U.S. states; or the buyer had already taken some of the goods, or had paid part of the price for which there was a written memorandum.

The Uniform Sales Act Statute of Frauds

This provision, with slight changes, was enacted in many states. In most states, however, the Uniform Sales Act was passed, and Section 4 of this act replaced the older provisions of the Statute of Frauds.

In recent years many states have adopted yet another act, the

Uniform Commercial Code. This act is similar to the Uniform Sales Act in that it attempts to make existing law uniform in all the states; however, the effects of the code are more extensive. In some states the U.C.C. has made significant changes in previous law, and covers far more than just the sale of goods. In most states, this code has replaced the Uniform Sales Act; therefore, in discussing this section of the Statute of Frauds, we will first look at the Uniform Sales Act and then at the Uniform Commercial Code.

The Uniform Sales Act states that contracts for the sale of goods, as well as those for the sale of choses in action must be in writing. (*Choses in action* are mostly saleable contract rights.) For example, suppose you and I make a contract whereby I am to mow your lawn every two weeks and, at the end of the summer, you are to pay me $50. The summer goes by, and I faithfully mow the lawn. Then I sell Fred my right to be paid for mowing the lawn. I have sold him a chose in action. Other kinds of choses in action are I.O.U.'s, securities, patent rights, and insurance policies. Contracts for the sale of these choses must be in writing if they are sold for more than the dollar limit specified in the Uniform Sales Act.

The Dollar Limit

This limit, which cannot be exceeded if an oral contract is to be enforced, varies greatly from state to state, ranging from as little as $30 in some states to as much as $12,500 in others. The value of the goods is the selling price established by the contract. If there is no mention of price in the contract, the court will take evidence as to the fair market value of the goods.

Receipt and Acceptance

The Uniform Sales Act also provides that an oral contract for the sale of goods can be enforced if the buyer receives and accepts part of the goods to be sold under the contract. This means that the buyer must have taken possession of the goods, and must also have accepted them. A buyer accepts goods either by telling the seller that they are satisfactory and that he will take them, or by showing by his actions that he will keep the goods; for example, by reselling the merchandise or by holding it for a long time.

Partial Payment

Oral contracts for the sale of goods can be enforced if the buyer has paid all or part of the agreed price or has made a down payment. Any payment which is made by the purchaser to the seller, however, must be regarded by both parties as partial payment for those particular goods. If, for example, the buyer owes the seller money on an entirely different contract, the remittance might be to pay that debt—not for the goods in the present oral contract. If the buyer sends a check, an I.O.U., or a bank draft, it is accepted as payment only if the seller considers the check or draft itself to be payment. If the seller considers the check to be only an assurance of later payment, that is, a security deposit, then the contract must be in writing. For example: I agree to sell you a car for $3,000. You give me a check for $500, and I state that the check is partial payment for the automobile; then the contract (even if oral) would be enforceable because you made part-payment. On the other hand, if in an oral contract I take your check but state that I will not count it as payment or let you have the car until I am certain the check is good, such an oral agreement could not be enforced. The reason is that your check was not meant as immediate part-payment.

Payment may be made in goods or in money. For example, I orally agree to give you 50 bushels of potatoes in exchange for 100 jars of jelly. If I then give you 10 bushels of potatoes, our oral contract is enforceable since the 10 bushels count as part-payment.

Specifically Made Goods

The contract for the sale of goods need not be in writing if the seller has already manufactured the articles to the buyer's specifications and if they are not suitable for sale to anyone else. The reason is that it would be unfair to allow the buyer to refuse goods on an oral contract where the seller has spent time and money making the goods on special order and then is stuck with them because they were designed specifically for one particular customer.

Finally, contracts for the sale of goods often provide for the seller to furnish labor as well as goods. What does a court do when a contract involves both services and merchandise? Generally, courts have decided that the contract was either basically for labor and, therefore, did not have to be in writing, or else that it was basically for goods and had to be in writing. Although courts differ in deciding what makes a contract basically for labor or for goods, common judicial practice has been to regard these combination agreements as service contracts. This is in line with the general reaction of the courts to the Statute of Frauds, and shows again how judicial bodies have tried to limit its application.

The Uniform Sales Act supports this tendency by providing that contracts in which goods are to be custom-made for a buyer need not be in writing. This provision, in actual practice, covers most of the contracts which involve both goods and labor. For example, if John promises to build a fence around Marsha's garden and to furnish the lumber with which to build it, the contract involves goods and labor. Furthermore, it falls within the provision of The Uniform Sales Act regarding goods made especially for a particular buyer; the contract cannot be resold.

The Uniform Commercial Code

The changes which the Uniform Commercial Code makes in the Statute of Frauds are still not entirely resolved because in most states the code is relatively new. It remains to be seen how the courts will interpret it; however, several things can be observed.

The Uniform Commercial Code has Statute of Frauds provisions dealing with sales in four subsections. Section 2-201 makes provision for contracts involving the sale of goods. This provision is slightly narrower than the one in the Uniform Sales Act since goods do not include choses in action, discussed earlier in this chapter.

This section of the code requires that contracts be in writing unless goods are custom-made and cannot be resold. This is similar to the Uniform Sales Act, except that the seller must have begun making the special goods or have committed himself to buying the raw materials for the merchandise before the oral contract becomes enforceable. Under the Uniform Sales Act, this is not necessary. An example will illustrate how this provision in the code works: I contract to build a fence around your garden and to buy the lumber for it. Under the Uniform Sales Act, I can have this contract enforced, even though it is not in writing. Under the Uniform Commercial Code, I cannot enforce this oral contract until I have either started building the fence or committed myself to buying the lumber for it.

Under the code, oral contracts for the sale of goods can also be enforced if the buyer pays for the goods, and the seller accepts the payment, or if the buyer receives and accepts the goods. These exceptions to the Statute of Frauds are very similar to those in the Uniform Sales Act.

Finally, the code provides an additional exception to the Statute of Frauds—one which is not in the Uniform Sales Act: a written agreement is not necessary if the party who is asserting the Statute of Frauds admits in court that a contract for the sale of goods was made. For example: suppose John contracted to sell Marsha a new car. The contract is not in writing. Marsha takes the car but refuses to pay for it. John sues, and Marsha claims that because their contract was not in writing, the Statute of Frauds makes their agreement unenforceable. If she has admitted in court that there was an agreement, she loses; for John can enforce it even though it is not in writing. If, however, she denies that there ever was an agreement, and claims that the Statute of Frauds prevents John from trying to make up an oral contract, she wins. This would work in reverse as well; that is, if John had taken Marsha's payment and then refused to give her the car.

Section 1-206 of the code supplements Section 2-201 by including choses in action. The most important feature in this Statute of Frauds provision is that it contains no exceptions. Contracts covered by Section 1-206 must be in writing, whether the buyer has made a payment or not. The suggested dollar limit, before a written contract becomes compulsory, however, is much higher than in Section 2-201.

The third place in the Uniform Commercial Code containing a Statute of Frauds provision is in Section 8-319 which covers contracts for the sale of stocks and bonds. There is no dollar limit in the provision, and all contracts for the purchase or sale of stock must be in writing. Again, however, such contracts need not be in writing if the buyer has made part-payment or has accepted the securities. The contract can be enforced only up to the amount the buyer has paid, or the value of the securities he has accepted. An oral contract to sell securities is also enforceable if the person trying to escape enforcement admits that a contract exists.

The final Statute of Frauds provision in the Uniform Commercial Code is in Section 9-203. This covers sales which create security interests. An example of a security interest would be a mutual agreement between buyer and seller for the purchase of a new car on the installment plan. Since the seller wants to protect himself in case the purchaser goes bankrupt, the sales contract will stipulate that failure to keep up with the payments is cause for repossession of the automobile. The seller then has what is called a security interest in the car, and should the buyer fail to meet the payments, the seller has the right to recover the car.

Whenever such security interests arise in a contract for the sale of goods, the Statute of Frauds requirement, in Section 9-203 of the Uniform Commercial Code, applies to them. This section requires that the security interest be detailed in writing and describe exactly what property is held, subject to the seller's security interest. For example: when you buy a car on time, the contract must describe the car in which the seller has a security interest so that a court can distinguish it from any other car.

Memoranda

In the previous subsection, it was pointed out that the Sale of Goods section of the Statute of Frauds required a written contract unless one of four conditions existed:

1. The price of the goods was less than a certain amount;
2. The buyer had already taken and accepted the goods;
3. The buyer had already paid for part or all of the goods; or
4. The person seeking enforcement of the contract could produce a written *memorandum* (a document in writing which is less formal than, and usually preliminary to, a contract).

A memorandum can make both contracts for the sale of goods and oral contracts, which come under the other provisions of the Statute of Frauds, enforceable. In other words, if there is a written memorandum of a contract in consideration of marriage, or of a contract for the sale of an interest in land, or of a promise to pay another's debts, these oral agreements are enforceable.

The Uniform Commercial Code makes important changes in the kind of memorandum required. When we talk about the

Sale of Goods section of the Statute of Frauds, the code applies only to sales of goods, choses in action, and security interests.

For example, a memorandum might be a hastily written note saying, "I hereby confirm an agreement to buy a bushel of apples from Jim." [*signed*] "Marsha." It might be a letter from one of the contracting persons to the other, noting the existence of a contract, or it may be a sales slip.

If it is to make the contract enforceable, a memorandum must be signed by the person charged; that is, the one who claims that no contract exists. For example, if I agree to sell you a bushel of apples, I could not use a memorandum to make you pay for them unless you had signed the memorandum. Similarly, you could not enforce the contract against me unless you could produce a memorandum with my signature on it.

The memorandum does not have to be a detailed description of the contract. On the other hand, it must contain the essential elements of the contract. (It is difficult to say in every circumstance exactly what these essential elements are, because this depends on what kind of contract is involved or who the contracting parties are.) Generally speaking, the more that the general circumstances support the existence and terms of a contract, the less specific and less complete the memorandum need be. It must identify the people on both sides of the contract. It need be signed only by the party who denies the existence of a contract, but it must name, or clearly identify, the other person in the contract.

In Chapter 5, we discussed the idea of consideration. Must the memorandum include a statement of the consideration? The answer is sometimes; in some states it is always compulsory while in others it is not.

The time when the memorandum was written is irrelevant. It can have been made either before or after an agreement was reached, as long as it was signed by the person against whom it is being used.

In finishing our examination of the memorandum, let us look at the memorandum requirements for the sale of goods in the

Uniform Commercial Code. Section 2-201, which covers the sale of goods, requires that the memorandum be signed by the person who is to be charged. The writing must also indicate the existence of a contract of sale. It need not include all the terms of the contract and it may incorrectly state a term. On the other hand, it must contain the quantity of goods to be sold, and it is enforceable only regarding the amount of the goods mentioned. If both buyer and seller are merchants, however, these requirements are not always necessary. That is, in some cases a memorandum does not have to be signed by the person against whom it is used. If one merchant sends a written confirmation of a contract to another, and if that confirmation would be a good memorandum against the sender, then the sender can enforce it against the recipient—even if that person never signed it. However, the recipient can object within ten days to the contents of the memorandum. For example: a wholesaler of sporting goods and a retail store owner agree over the phone to sell and buy 1,000 golf balls. The next day, the retailer sends a letter to the wholesaler confirming the contract for the sale of 1,000 golf balls. The store owner signs it "J. Retailer." If the retailer refuses to go through with the contract, this written confirmation is enough of a memorandum to enforce the contract against him. It establishes the existence of a contract, gives the quantity of goods to be sold, and is signed by the retailer. Normally, the memorandum could not be enforced against the wholesaler because he did not sign it. The Uniform Commercial Code says, however, that if the wholesaler does not object to the confirming letter within ten days of its receipt, the letter can be used to enforce a contract against him, even though the wholesaler does not sign it. Remember that this exemption applies only if the parties are merchants.

Section 1-206 covers contracts for the sale of personal property not covered by Section 2-201, mainly choses in action. A contract for the sale of this type of property cannot be enforced unless the memorandum fills four conditions:

1. It must be signed by the party against whom it is used.

2. It must give an indication that a firm contract exists.

3. It must reasonably identify what is to be sold.

4. It must indicate the price to be charged for the property.

Section 8-319 covers the sale of securities. A memorandum of a contract for the sale of securities is not enforceable unless it states both the price and quantity of stock to be sold and is signed by the party against whom it is used or by his agent or broker.

Miscellaneous

Sometimes a written contract does not accurately set forth the terms of the agreement between the parties. This can happen several ways:

1. One party may deceive the other, inducing him to sign a written contract that does not state clearly what the two of them have agreed upon.

2. The person drawing up the contract may make a mistake or a typing error.

3. Both parties may be mistaken about the contents of the contract.

In all three cases, a court would probably reform the written contract; that is to say, the court would treat the agreement as if it said exactly what the parties had really agreed on. This technique is used by the courts even where the actual contract is not in writing, in violation of the Statute of Frauds.

As we saw in the Sale of Goods section, a contract may be for both goods and labor. In other words, the Statute of Frauds would seem to require one part of the agreement to be in writing, but not the other. Similar difficulties may arise in regard to the other provisions of the Statute of Frauds. In deciding what to do in situations like this, the courts follow two general rules. First; if the contract can be divided into two parts without destroying the sense of each part, the court will do so. The portion that does not have to be in writing can then be enforced. For example; suppose John agreed with Marsha that he would sell her a car and mow her lawn. The agreement is not in writing. In such a case, the court would divide the contract into two parts—the lawn mowing and the car sale. It would not enforce the contract for the sale of the car, because the Sale of Goods section of the Statute of Frauds requires such contracts to be in writing. It would, however, enforce the contract for lawn mowing, because this is not required to be in writing.

Secondly; if, on the other hand, the two parts of the contract are so closely entwined that they cannot be separated without making nonsense of the whole contract, then no portion of the contract will be enforced unless the whole agreement is in writing.

Finally, let us imagine a contract which, in accordance with the Statute of Frauds, is in writing. Even though this contract must be written, the parties can agree to cancel it without putting the cancellation into writing. Furthermore, they can alter it without putting the alterations in writing, as long as the subject matter of the revisions is not required by the Statute of Frauds to be in writing.

Parol Evidence

General

We will now take up the problem of unwritten, or *parol evidence* and the rules which govern its use in contract situations. We have already seen, in discussing the Statute of Frauds, that the law may require certain kinds of contracts to be in writing. However, several types of contracts, need not be in writing, although many of them do end up wholly, or at least partly written, principally because it is customary in formalizing contracts to put at least part of them down on paper. Every contract which is made by mail involves *writing* in the form of letters. Sales slips, purchase forms, baggage tickets, telegrams, and airplane tickets are all written evidence of a contract.

A parol evidence problem can arise whenever there is some writing involved in the contract. Simply stated, a series of rules has been established to resolve conflicts between what the contracting parties said and did, and what they wrote. The so-called Parol Evidence Rule determines when a court will allow a party to a contract to present evidence, other than the writing, which will change the meaning or supplement the terms.

The rule states that when two parties have made a written contract, its terms cannot be altered by external evidence, such as the speech or conduct of the parties. This rule exists in order to establish certainty in the finished contract which usually follows prolonged bargaining and the exchange of numerous offers and counteroffers. When the parties reach an agreement, some mechanism is needed, which will show at a later date the terms that should be enforced in the final contract and what terms were only negotiations. Furthermore, most people concur that writing and signing an agreement are more binding than merely shaking hands. Parties thus undertake writing a contract with an air of seriousness, attempting to eliminate any ambiguity about what is written down.

Although the Parol Evidence Rule would rule out unwritten evidence almost everytime there is a written contract, there are several exceptions to this rule. They involve:

1. The time period which the Parol Evidence Rule governs.
2. The completeness and validity of the writing.
3. Unclear words or clauses in the writing.

We will examine each of these exceptions in turn.

Time

The first important limitation of the Parol Evidence Rule is the time period of its validity. Simply stated, the Parol Evidence Rule says that once a contract is in writing, all previous contacts between the parties are to be regarded as nothing more than negotiations. Such negotiations, and whatever they involve, whether spoken or written, are not binding and cannot alter, contradict, or add to the terms of the written contract. The rule, however, does not apply to anything which is done *after* the writing was made.

Let us take an example. Suppose that on Monday, Marsha goes to a used car dealer to buy an auto. She talks to a salesman, and they agree that she will buy a certain car for $1,500. The following day she comes back and, after further discussion, they write up a contract in which Marsha agrees to buy the car for $1,700. At this point the Parol Evidence Rule says that the price is $1,700. Prior oral agreements are mere negotiations and cannot alter the terms of the written contract.

But suppose Marsha comes back again on Wednesday, and the salesman, suffering from a bad conscience, tells her that $1,700 is too high a price; he agrees to sell her the car for $1,200. If the salesman later denies he ever offered her the car for $1,200, and Marsha is forced to sue him, a court would allow Wednesday's oral agreement to be introduced in evidence to contradict the written contract—even though this later agreement was not in writing. This is allowed because Wednesday's agreement was made *after* the written contract.

Invalid or Incomplete Writing

As we have seen, a written contract will supersede anything that has gone before; previous words and actions cannot be used in court to alter the meaning of the writing. Now we must qualify that broad statement by saying that it is true *only* where the writing fulfills certain requirements. In order to invoke the Parol Evidence Rule (and thus exclude other evidence in the contract), a party must show that the written contract is a valid and complete statement of the agreement).

The reason for this is most easily understood by looking at

the situation from the point of view of a judge. A litigant comes before him, shows him a written contract and demands that the other party be compelled to carry out his part of the bargain. Furthermore, he objects to any alteration of the contract by outside evidence.

The judge, of course, will be hesitant in such circumstances, especially if the contract seems to be incomplete, invalid, or unfair on its face. All he knows about the written agreement is what appears in it. The writing may well be invalid; for example, the other party might have been fraudulently induced into signing it. Perhaps the writing is incomplete and contains only part of the bargain between the parties. Either the writing should not be enforced at all (the first case), or the written agreement is only part of the total bargain which should be enforced (the second).

In order to find out more about the bargain, the judge must listen to evidence outside the contract which concerns its formulation. This evidence is, by its nature, parol evidence, and if such testimony decisively shows that the contract is invalid, the writing will not be enforced. In other words, parol evidence can always be used to show the invalidity of a writing. There are many reasons for which a court may invalidate a written contract. To take our used car example again, suppose that Marsha and the salesman signed a written contract whereby she was to buy a particular car for $2,000. If certain conditions prevailed when Marsha signed the contract, a court would allow her to get out of it free and clear. For instance, if Marsha could prove that when she signed it, the salesman told her the car was a year old, whereas it was actually six years old, and she reasonably believed him, the contract would be invalid because of fraud. If she could show that she signed because the salesman threatened her, the contract would be invalid because of duress. If she could prove that she and the salesman agreed that the sale would take place as soon as she could sell her own car, and she had not yet done so, present performance on the written contract would be defeated because it was created subject to a condition which has not yet occurred. These are some conditions which can render performance under a contract invalid—sometimes the entire contract—and parol evidence can be used to show the presence of any of them.

Earlier we mentioned that unless a written contract is complete as well as valid, parol evidence is admissible to alter or defeat that agreement. The reason for this is clear: a written contract is not to be supplemented by outside evidence merely because it is the final agreement between the parties. If the contract is incomplete, it is not final, and a court will be doing grave injustice to one of the parties by enforcing only the written part of the bargain.

How does a court go about allowing parol evidence to supplement or modify a written agreement when the writing is not complete? This is a two-step process, and both steps must be kept clearly in mind. The court will first hear parol evidence in order to decide whether the writing is a complete *integration* of the parties' bargain; that is, whether the writing is or is not the complete agreement. When its completeness is called into question, a written instrument cannot be allowed to be sole proof of its own validity or completeness. Thus, even if the writing stated, "This writing is a complete statement of the contract between the parties," the court could discount it and turn to other outside evidence to aid in proving the matter. In this first step, note that the court does not allow the parol evidence to change the writing, but only to establish whether or not the writing is complete. On the basis of what it has heard, the court then decides whether the writing is, in fact, a complete integration. If it is, the matter ends there; for the writing stands and cannot be supplemented.

If, however, the court decides that the writing is not complete, it will then enter into the second phase of the process. At this point, the parties present parol evidence in order to prove what the unwritten parts of the contract were. One observation should be made at this point: although this two-step process is used by the courts, it is often hard to distinguish between the stages in actual practice. The reason is that the parties will use certain parol evidence in stage one, to show that the writing is not complete; often this is the same evidence that is used to supplement the writing in stage two. The identical nature of the evidence in both stages makes it hard to distinguish between them.

To clarify this point, suppose that Marsha and the salesman struck the following bargain: the salesman would sell the car for $1,500 but would give Marsha a credit of $500 for the trade-in value on her present auto. Then they draw up a contract stating that John Jones, salesman, agrees to sell Marsha Blake a 1963 Chevrolet for which she agrees to pay $1,500. When Marsha turns in her old car, she pays $1,000 and takes the 1963 Chevy. Then the salesman sues her for $500, claiming that only $1,000 of the $1,500 purchase price in the written contract has been paid. In court, during stage one, Marsha will attempt to show that the writing is not complete. To prove this, she will testify that she and the salesman had agreed orally on a purchase price of $1,500, less the $500 trade-in allowance for her old car. If the judge decides that her testimony proves the writing is incomplete, stage two will begin, and Marsha must then state what the unwritten terms of the contract were. Her testimony in this second phase will be identical to the evidence used in stage one.

When a writing is not complete and parol evidence is used to establish supplementary terms, these new terms cannot contradict anything in the writing. The reason is that where no fraud, duress, or mistake is involved, a court confronted by two conflicting statements—one oral, one written—will take the written one as being true because (1) the law wishes to encourage putting agreements into writing; and (2) it is much easier to lie about past oral statements than to alter written ones. Allowing oral evidence to contradict writing may induce perjury and deception.

The foregoing illustrates how the Parol Evidence Rule operates, but it fails to show how courts decide whether the writing is complete on the basis of the evidence presented in stage one. The writing may seem to be exhaustive and complete, but it may actually have been intended to be only partial. In such a case the parol evidence may indicate that the court should find out if an entirely separate and possibly valid oral contract exists. Deciding this issue depends largely upon the intention of the parties who may have meant the writing to be only part of their total transactions. In determining what their intention was, courts will consider several factors:

First, the circumstances surrounding the transaction. If the arrangement is normally only partly written, probably the parties intended the writing to be only partial. For example, if I sell you a dozen crates of vegetables and the only written portion of the contract is your purchase order, then it is simply a matter of your presenting a written order and my orally agreeing to sell. In such cases, any reservations or conditions which I may have placed upon the sale will not be found in the written purchase order. In a suit involving such circumstances, a court is apt to decide that the parties did not intend the writing to be complete.

Secondly, the courts will look at the purpose of the oral agreement and the writing, and if they find that the objective of the oral agreement is so far removed from the main purpose of the written contract that it would be natural for the parties to regard it as separate and not include it in the writing, a separate, oral contract will be found to exist. Thus, courts compare the subject matter of the writing and the subject matter of the oral agreement. If the oral agreement deals with a subject that is also covered by the writing, courts will conclude that the parties intended the writing to supersede the oral agreement. For example: a landlord rents a house, and the tenant signs a written lease which gives him the right to use the garden, the backyard, and the garage. If the tenant later tries to establish that there was an oral agreement that he could use the swimming pool, the Parol Evidence Rule would probably preclude his proving the latter point, unless he could show that the swimming pool was built *after* the lease was signed. The reason is that the writing seems to have positively covered all areas the tenant could use. Parol evidence on the same subject is not allowed to alter the writing, because the parties intended the writing to be final regarding the areas the tenant could use. It is quite clear that the purpose of the lease was to define the tenant's rights to use the property, and it would be illogical for the parties to have a separate agreement about the swimming pool.

Ambiguous Writing

Parol evidence can also modify a contract when the writing is unclear. Lack of clarity commonly occurs when an ambiguous word or phrase is used in a crucial part of the contract and any one of several meanings may have been intended. In such a case, parol evidence may be admitted to establish exactly what the parties meant by the equivocal word. For example: suppose that Marsha and the car salesman write a contract stating that the salesman agrees to sell a "brand new green Chevrolet Impala sedan" to Marsha for which she promises to pay $2,500. The words "brand new green Chevrolet Impala sedan" seem unequivocal. But suppose that the salesman removes the tires, armrests, mirrors, headlights, carburetor, and battery from the car before turning the car over to Marsha. It is still a "brand new green Chevrolet Impala sedan," and the writing does not indicate whether the car was supposed to have tires, battery, headlights, carburetor, and armrests. In this situation, Marsha would be allowed to present parol evidence as to what the parties meant by "brand new green Chevrolet Impala sedan" when they put those words into the contract.

In other cases, the writing may be unclear because it is based on certain trade practices and understandings. In such a case, parol evidence can be used to explain the implicit terms upon which the writing is based, even if that explanation has the effect of adding terms to the contract. For example; John imports figs from Persia; he is well established in this business and familiar with its practices. He makes a contract with Ali whereby John "agrees to buy two tons of June figs, for $1000, and Ali agrees to sell them." When John gets the figs, he discovers that 25 percent of them are spoiled. If he tries to sue Ali for damages, Ali is allowed to introduce parol evidence to show that 25 percent of *every* shipment of June figs are spoiled, that all fig merchants know this, and that the purchase price of June figs takes this fact into account. If Ali can prove this, it will stand, although, in effect, it adds another term to the contract— that the seller can only guarantee that 75 percent of the figs will be good.

Parol evidence, then, can be used to establish trade customs which explain the meaning of the written contract and which may even add terms to it. Courts allow this, however, only if the following conditions can be shown about the custom:

1. The custom must have been in use at the time the contract was made. The reason for this is that the parties obviously didn't make the contract with the custom in mind if it had not yet come into being.

2. For the same reason, the custom must be generally known and used in the trade, or else it must be shown that both parties to the contract knew of the custom's use and validity.

3. The custom must be legal. Thus, in the example of the fig merchant, if there were a law requiring that in contracts for the sale of figs the seller must guarantee the entire shipment, the custom would be illegal. In that case, the illegal trade custom, no matter how well established, could not alter the contract; to do so would be to allow custom to control the law.

4. The custom cannot directly contradict the writing. For example: if Ali had guaranteed 100 percent of the figs, and this had been written into the contract, the fact that trade custom is different would not have allowed a change in the contract.

7. Contract Interpretation

General

As WE saw in Chapter 6, in connection with the Statute of Frauds and the Parol Evidence Rule, courts have the power to modify and complete written contracts in certain situations. In this chapter we will examine the words used by the parties to express contractual agreements and the methods employed by the courts in trying to give meaning to the intent expressed by these words.

This chapter will also deal with cases in which courts refuse to enforce a new agreement, while in others they dissolve the contract entirely. In these situations, we will see how courts alter the language of an agreement, sometimes adding, sometimes deleting words, and occasionally doing both. The courts do this only under special circumstances: if a contract is unjust; if there is a mistake in the terms; or if both parties have erred in expressing the terms of the agreement.

The Words Themselves

The starting point for interpreting a contract must be the words themselves, as set forth in the text of the writing. A court thus looks at the words of the contract and tries to give them the meaning which the parties intended when they made the agreement. If that fails (which often happens, since the parties would not have come to court if the contract were unambiguous and its meaning clear), the court tries to attach the everyday meaning to the words; that is, the meaning that one would find in a nontechnical book or a dictionary.

In discussing the Parol Evidence Rule, however, we saw that people in certain trades will often apply particular meanings to certain words or terms. Courts will accept these trade definitions if the people who made the contract can show that they had these special meanings in mind. For example, in early nineteenth century England, the word "thousand," when used by those in the rabbit trade, actually meant 1,200 rabbits. Thus, if two parties in that business made a contract for a thousand rabbits, a court would interpret thousand to mean 1,200 because both parties would have known the terminology of their industry.

By interpreting according to trade custom, courts give the meaning to the words which the people who used them intended them to express. This is the primary rule which courts follow in interpreting contracts: they will attempt to establish what the parties sought to accomplish by making their bargain. Also, in examining particular words in dispute, the court will try to give them a meaning which is consistent with the general purpose of the contract. When the contract as a whole expresses a clear intent and the specific language in dispute can be made consistent with that intent, the matter is ended. But what happens when the language of the contract does not show a clear purpose? What if the disputed language can be interpreted several ways, and each is equally consistent with a possible general intent of the contract?

In such a case, courts will still attempt to give words the meaning which the parties intended them to have. But since the contract itself is unclear, they will look at the circumstances which surrounded the forming of the contract and at the actions of the parties. From the surrounding circumstances, the court will attempt to construct the purpose of the contract. Once the intent is established, the court can interpret the specific language of the contract in accordance with the agreement's general purpose—even eliminating conflicting or surplus words if necessary.

One difficulty which frequently arises is a conflict in meaning between two parts of the same contract. When this happens, the more specific and important portion of the instrument will be given greater weight. Courts allow a specific provision to prevail over a more general one on the ground that, as a rule, the specific stipulation was meant to carry more weight. For example: suppose that I contract to sell you canned peas, nuts, cereal, and fresh tomatoes. The contract says that you cannot return any of the goods for refund. A second provision, however, states that if the tomatoes spoil, you can get a refund on them. Should this happen, a court would probably give the second provision greater weight and allow you to get your money back for the tomatoes. The reason is that the general provision covered all the goods that were not likely to spoil; however, tomatoes are very perishable, and it is not likely that we had them in mind when we wrote the general provision. When we wrote the second provision, it is obvious that we were referring specifically to the tomatoes, and we decided that the bad ones could be returned.

Sometimes a word or a term in a contract may have two meanings. If one of the definitions makes the contract illegal, a court will always apply the meaning which makes the agreement legal, because the parties are presumed to be law-abiding people who would not intentionally make an illegal contract. Suppose, for example, that I contract to sell you ten head of cattle. There is a state law prohibiting the sale of diseased cattle; however, the word "cattle" in the contract could mean either "healthy cattle" or "any cattle, whatever their health." In this situation a court would choose the first meaning, thereby making the contract legal, and preventing my breaking the law by selling sick cattle.

Different parts of a contract may have several meanings. If only one meaning makes the different parts of the contract consistent, that is the purport the courts will take to be the correct one. If some of the meanings are unreasonable or unduly harsh, the courts will accept a fair or more reasonable reading as the true one. The reason, again, is that the law courts assume the parties are attempting to write a consistent contract and to deal fairly with one another. Otherwise, of course, courts would favor ambiguous contracts in which unscrupulous parties could insert unfair terms.

Sometimes only one of the two parties to a contract has decided on its form. Insurance policies are a good example of this; the insurer writes the contract and the man who buys the policy merely signs it. If a word or a term in this kind of a contract has more than one meaning, a court will generally use the definition which is favorable to the person who had no hand in writing the contract. Since one party had nothing to do with drafting the contract, great weight must be given to what he thought the words in the document meant when he signed it. Since the insurance carrier had complete control over the words used, the company is responsible for making sure that their meaning is clear and completely understood by the other party. If their meaning is unclear, the court will interpret the terms according to what the other party to the contract asserts—if this meaning is a reasonable one. This rule applies to both written and oral contracts. For example, I make an oral offer to you, and you accept it. If the words which I used in the offer were ambiguous, a court will apply the meaning least favorable to me.

Some contracts consist of large sections of printed text to which typed clauses are added. Again, insurance policies are a good example. Most policies are printed forms to which additional clauses or revisions are typed or written in. If the printed section of such a contract conflicts with the written or typed portion, the latter part will prevail because it was written with a specific person in mind just before that party signed the contract.

Words Added by the Court

When contracts are incomplete, unjust, intentionally inconsistent, or ambiguous, courts may decide to abandon part or all of the existing written agreement and substitute what they feel to have been the intended bargain between the parties. Lawyers and judges, when speaking of contracts to which the courts have added words and terms, call them *implied contracts*. Implied contracts can be *implied in fact* or *implied in law*. This distinction, while not always very clear in actual practice, is useful and worth an explanation.

Contracts Implied in Fact

These are agreements in which a court examines the surrounding circumstances and the actions of the parties and, based on this information, decides that a promise or a bargain has been made. This promise will be enforced even though the contracting parties never agreed upon those words or terms.

Contracts implied in fact most frequently arise in cases which involve an offer with an improper or absent acceptance. Courts imply an acceptance by the offeree because of his activities, even though there has been no proper acceptance, and the offeree, therefore, becomes bound by the contract.

A typical case occurs when a person who received an offer remains silent. If this person has accepted similar contracts in the past without ever giving written or oral assent, courts are likely to imply an acceptance. For example: suppose I have offered to plow your driveway whenever it snows. Although you never agreed explicitly to my offer, in the past you always gave me $10 after I had finished. Now if you suddenly refuse to pay me, a court is very likely to find implied acceptance because of your behavior on all the previous occasions.

An even more important factor that leads courts to imply an acceptance arises when one person receives benefit without having to pay for it, and the other party suffers a loss because he expected to be paid. This factor is present in the previous example, for I spent time and energy plowing your driveway— all to my detriment, expecting that you would pay me for it. Such a situation is unjust, and courts are usually quite willing to allow a person compensation for his efforts after he has spent time and money fulfilling an offer.

A somewhat less clear-cut case results when one person does lose time and money, but the other person receives no benefits in return. It is more difficult to see why the second person should pay when that person did not get any benefits. Nonetheless courts are still inclined to make the second person pay.

Suppose that I offer to shovel your walk when it snows, and you do not reply. Assuming that your silence means "yes," I go out and buy a snowplow, solely for the purpose of clearing your walk. In this case, you have received no benefit because your walk hasn't been cleared yet; but on the other hand, I have gone to the expense of purchasing a snowplow. Under these circumstances a court would be unlikely to award me compensation for my purchase of the machine, especially since its cost is high in relation to the cost of clearing a walk and because my loss is not permanent; that is, I can either sell the snowplow or find other walks to clear.

Finally, there are several cases in which courts have implied an acceptance even though the person who made the offer suffered no direct loss, and the other party gained no direct benefits. These cases are based on the premise that the first person, although he suffered no loss, was done out of anticipated profits. Recovery in this type of case is even less likely than in the two preceding examples. Generally speaking, situations of this kind will occur whenever the actions of one person reasonably lead another party to believe that a contract exists between them, and when the second person, believing that a contract is in existence, does things which cause him to suffer loss.

Contracts Implied in Law

Among the most common contracts are what lawyers call *quasi-contracts* which are created by the courts even though the parties involved did not actually make a contract. The court creates these contracts because not to do so would be unfair. Since the reason for doing so is to prevent injustice, however, it must be remembered that a court will not create a quasi-contract if there is any other fair solution to the problem.

Generally speaking, a court will create a quasi-contract only if two things have happened:

1. If one person has received a benefit because of something another person does for him.

2. If the first person has unfairly enjoyed these benefits without paying for them.

Some examples will show how this works. There is a heavy snowfall, and you cannot get your car out of the garage. I plow your driveway while you stand by and say nothing. In this situation a court may or may not create a quasi-contract. You have received a benefit, but it is not clear whether it would be unfair for you to keep the benefit. If I had done the shoveling as a gift to you, it would not be unfair for you to keep the benefit without paying for it. If, on the other hand, I never shoveled snow except for pay, and if I had indicated that I expected to get paid for what I was doing, it would be unfair of you to get the benefit without paying. In such a case, a court might well create a quasi-contract. If we remember the snow shoveling example in the subsection, "Contracts Implied in Fact," we can see that this situation is almost the same. The only difference is technical: here a court would say that it was creating an entire contract where none had existed; in the example cited in the previous subsection, the court would say that, from your conduct, it implied an acceptance to my offer.

Suppose there is a snowfall, and I plow your driveway while you are away. In such a case, a court would probably not create a quasi-contract because you neither asked for my services nor had you the chance to agree, even by silence. The benefit was forced on you without your knowledge and, under the circumstances, it would not be unfair for you to retain the benefit without compensating me.

When a quasi-contract is created because someone receives an unpaid-for benefit the person who conferred the benefit is allowed to get back, at most, the value of the benefit. This is an important point, because in many cases the value of the benefit to the recipient will differ from the expense incurred by the person who gave the benefit. For example: suppose that the benefit to you of having your driveway plowed is $10. Suppose, however, that John spent a dollar in carfare getting to your house, $35 for a plow that he would not have bought otherwise, and two hours shoveling, which is worth $4 to him. If the court created a quasi-contract between John and you, it would allow John only $10, since that is the worth of the benefit he conferred on you. The fact that shoveling cost John $40 would be irrelevant.

Many quasi-contract cases involve the Statute of Frauds. The statute makes certain unwritten contracts unenforceable; for instance, contracts involving the sale of land and agreements whose performance takes longer than one year. Therefore, if the contract is not in writing, no contract exists between the parties and the court creates a quasi-contract. These cases are similar to those where unwritten contracts are enforced because one person has completed his side of the bargain; they differ, however, in one respect—if the court creates a quasi-contract, the party who has been wronged can recover only the value of the benefit he gave to the other person. If the court enforces an unwritten contract, however, both parties get what they would have received under the terms of the contract, had it been written.

Quasi-contracts are also created in cases dealing with the performance of services in emergencies. For example: a doctor witnesses an auto accident, and then treats the unconscious victims. The injured people have not made a contract with the doctor, but a court will sometimes create a quasi-contract to compensate the doctor for the value of the services he rendered.

Warranty of Title

Warranties also lead courts to imply or add terms. (A *warranty* is a guarantee by the seller or manufacturer of the quality, durability, and performance of a service or appliance.) The seller warrants that the goods are free of defects and suitable for a certain type of use. A warranty implied in law obligates the merchant to protect consumers against potentially dangerous, undetected defects in equipment. Today warranties are usually codified into statutes. Since the Uniform Commercial Code contains such a codification, and has been adopted in 49 states, we will limit our discussion of warranties implied in law to those examples in the code. Warranties implied in law in all states will not necessarily be exactly the same as those in the code; nevertheless, those in the code give an idea of the breadth and coverage of implied warranties in general.

The first warranty in the code is in Section 2-312. It says that a seller of goods warrants that he has good title to them and that there are no *outstanding encumbrances* on the goods, except those of which the buyer has knowledge. (*Encumbrances* are unpaid taxes, installments, security interests, or mortgages.) This means that if I sell you a car, I guarantee that I own it free and clear before selling it to you even though I may not have specified this in the contract. Thus, if I had stolen the car, I would have broken the warranty, and, if the police recovered the stolen car from you, you could get your money back from me. If you know that I have not paid the entire amount due on the car, there is no problem, since we could arrange for you to continue the payments and deduct the unpaid balance from the amount you pay me. On the other hand, if you are unaware of money owed, and the finance company repossesses the car from you, you can get your money back from me. The foregoing warranties are not automatically created, however. They are employed only when there is nothing to the contrary in the contract or in the circumstances surrounding the contract. For example: if I put into the contract a sentence stating that I did not warrant that there were no encumbrances on the car, these warranties would not be implied and, therefore, you could not recover the purchase price from me, after losing the car to the finance company.

The circumstances surrounding the sale can also prevent these warranties from arising, especially if they give the buyer good reason to believe that the seller does not claim to own what he is selling.

Warranty of Merchantability

The *warranty of merchantability*, another implied warranty set forth in the Uniform Commercial Code, is in Section 2-314. It says that a merchant, whenever he sells goods and despite the fact that he may not say so in the contract of sale, guarantees that the goods are merchantable. To be a merchant, a seller must be a person who usually sells goods of the kind in question; that is, he is in the business. For example, a used car dealer is a merchant when he sells used cars, but would not be a merchant for the purpose of selling his lawn mower to his next door neighbor. A person who runs a hardware store is a merchant when he sells a lawn mower, but is not when he sells his car to a party who responds to his newspaper ad.

A merchant, then, warrants that goods are merchantable when he sells them. Section 2-314 goes on to list the minimum requirements of merchantability:

1. Goods must conform to the description in the contract, according to the standard of the trade.

2. Fungible goods (interchangeable items like nails or hair-pins) should be of fair-to-average quality, and must serve the purpose for which they were purchased. The opposite of fungible goods are objects such as houses; if someone buys a home, he purchases a specific house and would be unhappy if the seller tried to substitute a different house. A merchant who sells uniform goods like bobby pins, which are interchangeable, warrants at least that they will be of fair and average quality.

3. The goods must be fit for the ordinary purposes to which they are usually put. Thus, a car dealer warrants that the automobiles he sells are suitable for driving in city traffic, since that is an ordinary way of using a car. He does not warrant, however, that his cars are fit for driving in a jungle.

4. Different units of a single lot of goods sold together must be of similar "kind, quality, and quantity." For example, if I sold you 100 boxes of bobby pins at two dollars per box, I would have to warrant that the bobby pins in any box are of a quality comparable to that of the bobby pins in any other box; furthermore, that the bobby pins will all be of the same style or kind; and, finally, I would warrant that there are roughly the same number of bobby pins in each box. Exactly how similar the units must be, however, depends on the amount of variation that the contract of sales or the custom of the trade allow.

5. The goods must be adequately contained, packaged, and labelled.

6. The goods must satisfy any promises which are made on the label of their container.

This section of the code also provides that other warranties of merchantability may arise from the custom of the trade. This provision allows the court wide latitude in dealing with warranties of merchantability. If it finds that vendors in a particular trade customarily guarantee standards of durability or performance on certain articles of merchandise, a court may create that same warranty in a sale even if the seller did not actually make such a warranty.

In summary, then, a merchant warrants that his goods are

merchantable, even if he does not explicitly say so in the contract of sale. By so guaranteeing, he warrants, at least, that they will be of a quality generally accepted in the trade; that fungible goods will be of fair-to-average quality; that the goods are suitable for ordinary usage; that different units of a sale will not vary in quality, number, or kind; that the merchandise is properly packaged and labelled and will do what the label promises.

Warranty of Fitness

Section 2-315 sets up a second implied warranty, which is called a *warranty of fitness* for a particular purpose. This warranty, which applies not only to merchants, but to anyone who sells goods, compels the seller to warrant the fitness of the goods he sells for a particular purpose—even though he says nothing to that effect.

This warranty is read into the contract by the court only when: (1) the seller knows, or has good reason to believe he knows, to what use the buyer is going to put the goods, and (2) the seller has reason to know that the buyer is depending on his (the seller's) skill. If the seller knows, or has good reason to know, both these things, courts find he has warranted the goods as fit for the purpose to which the buyer is going to put them.

For example: John is an expert mechanic and car salesman, and Fred, a fur trapper from northern Canada, comes to him. Fred tells John that he knows nothing about automobiles. He has heard that John is an authority on cars and he trusts John to give him what he needs. Fred explains that he wants a car which he can use in fur trapping, one capable of travel over rough country roads. This is a case in which John would make a warranty of fitness when he sold Fred the car. However, if Fred brought his cousin, an automotive engineer, with him, no warranty of fitness for a particular purpose would be implied. The reason is that Fred had not given John good reason to believe that he was relying on John's knowledge. In this case, there is no reason to make John warrant fitness for Fred's purpose, when the latter has not asked his advice and is, instead, depending on his cousin's expertise.

Section 2-316 of the Uniform Commercial Code explains how implied warranties of merchantability can be changed or eliminated. An implied warranty of merchantability is eliminated or altered only where the seller says that he makes no warranties, and specifically uses the word merchantability. If the seller tries to change or eliminate an implied warranty of merchantability, the writing in the contract must mention merchantability conspicuously. Thus, a seller can change or eliminate a warranty of fitness only by putting his refusal to warrant into writing and, even then, he will succeed only if the writing is conspicuous.

Warranties of merchantability and fitness can also be eliminated by words which make it clear that no warranties of any kind are given. Thus, if the seller tells the buyer, "You're taking it with all faults," or "I'm selling it as is," no warranties may be created.

Implied warranties are also eliminated when the buyer inspects the goods before he decides to buy. The seller is not held to make any warranties regarding defects that the buyer should have discovered in his inspection prior to purchase. Suppose you, knowing little about cars, go into an automobile showroom and examine a car. After deciding to buy it, you notice that the upholstery has a large, obvious tear in it. The dealer has not broken any warranty if he sells you the car which you examined, since you should have found the damage during your inspection. But suppose instead that the transmission is defective. The dealer has then breached an implied warranty of merchantability, since you could not have discovered a defect of this kind in a superficial examination of the car, especially if your knowledge of cars is minimal.

Miscellaneous

Warranties and quasi-contracts are not the only situations in which courts have inserted into contracts terms and conditions to which the parties never explicitly agreed. Courts imply extra promises in a contract where it is necessary to rectify an extremely unjust bargain; for example, where it is apparent that one of the parties is attempting to gain an unfair advantage on a technicality. Thus, courts often imply a promise that one party will not hinder the other from performing his duty under the contract. Suppose John contracts with Marsha to build a house, which he promises to complete by August 1st. If the house is not finished by that date, John promises to do all the remaining work free of charge. Marsha, with not the most admirable intentions, has a barrier built across the road to her land, making it impossible for John even to begin the house before August 1st. There is nothing in the contract stating that Marsha cannot do this. Nevertheless, a court would certainly create an implied promise on her part not to interfere with John's work on the house.

Courts also frequently imply promises when something unexpected happens which greatly alters the contractual bargain. For example: John makes a contract to rent his theater to Marsha for the evening of August 1st. On July 30, the theater burns down. Marsha sues John for breaking the contract, since he promised to rent her the theater, and when August 1st came, he refused. In this case, a court will insert a term into the contract which bases John's promise to rent the theatre on the condition that the theater exists. In other words, while John actually said that he would rent his theater on August 1st, the court creates an implied promise which states that he will rent his theater on August 1st if on that date it is still standing.

Limiting Contractual Terms

We have seen how courts may imply extra words and promises in a contract, although they were never actually made. More surprising is the fact that they will occasionally imply words and terms which not only did not exist in the contract, but which also flatly contradict what has been written in the contract. The written terms of the contract are replaced by the bargain which the court establishes. Generally speaking, courts have done this because the language of the contract creates an extremely unjust arrangement. If one party to the contract had a very powerful bargaining position and forced the other party to enter into the unfair agreement, or if, as in the previous example, something unexpected happened which drastically altered the contractual situation, the court could rewrite the contract. The courts seek primarily to minimize the unfairness, while keeping the contract as close to the original as possible. Thus, implied warranties may be created although the contract specifically recites that there are no warranties; implied conditions may be inserted in such a way that the actual promises in the contract are gravely limited (as illustrated by the last example in which the theater burned down).

Conditions

A *condition* in a contract is a stipulation stating that one party will have to perform something when a certain circumstance or event occurs. Like warranties, conditions can be added to a contract by the court to correct an unjust or mistaken situation, and, for that reason, they are discussed here. Examples of conditions showing the various ways they may operate are: (1) If it snows, I will shovel your walk. (2) I will not shovel your walk unless it snows more than three inches. In each of these cases the condition upon which my performance depends is snow; and the performance, dependent upon the conditions, is shoveling your walk.

There are some peculiarities about how courts treat conditions which make their interpretation slightly different and a bit troublesome. The first difficulty is in establishing the existence of the condition itself; courts may create a condition in a contract if they feel it is essential, although the express words may contain no mention of the condition. Sometimes the reverse occurs, and an express condition will be wiped out if it is unjust or unreasonable. A brief digression into the way courts interpret contracts will help to explain the circumstances under which conditions are created or expunged by the courts.

There are two ways in which courts interpret the meaning of a contract: (1) The court takes the express words of a contract and, in accordance with certain rules, decides what those words mean. This is referred to as interpreting the express *provisions* of a contract; and (2) By what is called *implication*. A court will add something to the contract which the agreement itself does not include. Implication, as we have already seen, if of two kinds: things *implied in fact* which the court adds to a contract *because of the actions of the parties* to the contract; and *things implied in law*, whereby a court adds to the agreement in order to do justice to the parties, irrespective of their actions. Conditions in a contract can be either express (those written into a contract or agreed upon orally), or constructive (those created by a court). Express conditions may also be added to the contract in the event that the actions of the parties prove that they intended a condition to be in the contract even though they didn't actually say it or insert it into the writing. *Express conditions* are equivalent to "implied in fact;" *constructive conditions* are those which a court creates and adds to a contract irrespective of its language or the intention of the parties. Constructive conditions, therefore, are equivalent to the term "implied in law," as discussed earlier in Chapter 7.

Besides the classifications express or constructive, conditions are also referred to as *precedent, concurrent,* and *subsequent.*

These classifications have to do with the timing of the condition and the duty connected with the condition. A condition *precedent* must occur *before* a party is required to perform. (For example, a condition which says "John will shovel Marsha's walk if it snows" is a condition precedent.) John is not obligated to do anything until it snows. In other words, the condition, a snowfall, must come first, and only then is John required to perform. Conversely, if John refuses to shovel, he will be breaking the contract only if it has already snowed.

A condition *subsequent* is one whose occurrence excuses one party from performing a duty that had been required under the contract. An example of a condition subsequent would be: John will shovel Marsha's walk next week, but if it does not snow, then he is excused from shoveling. John has a present obligation. The condition has not occurred yet, and only after the week has elapsed without a snowfall will John be excused from shoveling. Should it snow, however, and if he refuses to shovel, he will be breaking the contract.

In a condition *precedent,* then, Marsha is not entitled to anything, and John cannot break the contract during the period before the condition occurs. In a condition *subsequent,* Marsha is already entitled to something, and John remains obligated to her under the contract until the condition occurs.

This classification of conditions is important in that once it is decided whether a condition is precedent or subsequent, courts can determine if the contract was broken, and which party was responsible for the breach. This may be important in settling the dispute, as we will see in Chapter 8 in which contract breaches are discussed in detail.

Finally, some conditions are called *concurrent.* An example of a concurrent condition would be John's promise to shovel Marsha's walk, and her promise to pay him two dollars. John does not have to perform unless he gets paid. On the other hand, Marsha does not have to pay unless John shovels. One promise is contingent on the other, and they must be performed at the same time. Lawyers call such promises concurrent conditions.

8. Dissolution and Breach of Contract – Remedies

General

In this Chapter we will examine two occurrences which often give rise to disputes between the parties to a contract. The first situation results from a mistake made by one or both parties on the formation of a contract. The other occurs when performance under the contract becomes impossible or extraordinarily difficult.

We will then see how these two events affect the rights and duties of the people involved. This, in turn, will give us a reasonable idea of what a court does when such occurrences lead to litigation.

Next, a subject called *discharge* will be examined. Discharge occurs when one party to a contract is relieved of all duties under that contract. We have already encountered one example of discharge; when a condition is not fulfilled, the party whose performance depends upon that condition is relieved of all duties under the agreement. We will now look at others.

The last two sections of this chapter are closely linked: the first deals with a breach which occurs when a party obligated under a contract fails to perform. (Again, we have already seen examples of breach; for instance, the failure to fulfill a condition.) There are many ways to breach a contract and the legal

102

consequences arising from various kinds of breach differ considerably.

The classification and application of these legal consequences to different types of breach is called *remedies*. When a court decides a case, it must look for the fairest and best settlement between the parties. Often a court is limited in its selection of remedies, however, and cannot simply command the loser to do whatever it thinks most just because the *courts'* powers are limited.

Often, courts make the losing party pay the winner, or they may sometimes order him to do something, for example, to render performance according to the contract. In general, the amount a court makes the losing party pay and the orders which the law is prepared or empowered to give him are determined by the nature of the breach committed. For this reason, the subjects of remedies and breach are closely interwoven.

In the section on remedies, therefore, we will look at the different powers a court may use to correct faulty performance or failure to perform. Furthermore, we will see what limits exist on the remedial powers of a court.

Mistakes

Mistakes of Fact

People often make mistakes when they are in the process of forming or executing contracts. These are usually mistakes of fact in that they involve incorrect ideas about the existence, nature, or identity of a physical object, person, or contractual term. In this subsection we shall discuss this kind of mistake.

If only one of the parties to the contract makes the mistake, it is of crucial importance to ascertain why he blundered. If the mistake was made because of carelessness, such an error is obviously treated differently than one which occurs despite the exercise of great care by the party.

Many factual mistakes result from misunderstandings arising during the making of a contract. For this reason courts often dispose of such cases by applying the rules of offer and accept- ance. These rules were set forth in Chapter 7, but require re- examination insofar as they apply to mistakes.

Most factual mistakes occur when a man makes an offer, thinking its meaning is exact and clear to the other party. An- other person accepts the offer, but misinterprets the meaning of a term. For example: I tell you, "I will sell you a bike for $50," and you answer, "Sold." In making the offer I intended to sell you an old, dilapidated bicycle, while you, in accepting it, thought that you were buying a new racing bike. In such a case, courts hold that no contract was formed, because my offer—as I meant it—was never validly accepted. Agreement on the sub- ject matter of the contract was never reached and, therefore, no contract exists.

Other factors present may be important, however, and may change the result; one such factor is carelessness. If the circum- stances show that I was careless in making my offer and led you to think that you were to get the racing bike, a court might well say that a contract exists, and that by my misleading con- duct, I had bound myself to sell the racing bike. Whether I was sufficiently careless depends a good deal upon what the court thinks you should reasonably have believed from my conduct. If a court decides that a normal person in your position would have thought he was getting a racing bike, then the court is likely to award you the better bicycle.

Your conduct is also important. In accepting my offer, you must do or believe what a reasonable person would in the same situation; that is, you cannot act carelessly. If my offer is ambiguous, and you misunderstand it only because you are careless, a court will usually decide that no contract exists or the contract must be enforced according to the way that I understood it. You must also act honestly. If the circumstances surrounding my offer should make it obvious that I could not possibly intend to sell a racing bike for such a low price, a court will uphold the contract according to my meaning.

Another factor affecting such a mistake of fact is the importance of the error. In the previous example, the mistake is rather important, since the racing bicycle is obviously worth much more. Ordering me to sell a racing bike for $50 may cause me great hardship. On the other hand, if both you and I had interpreted the word "bike" to mean "racing bicycle," but I had intended to sell a bicycle with red reflectors while you had expected one with yellow reflectors, the mistake is not of great importance. Ordering me to sell you what you thought you had purchased will not harm me greatly. In this case, courts are much more willing to enforce the contract against me.

Another common contractual mistake involves the identity of a party to the contract. Cases involving this sort of mistake are also often looked at from the standpoint of offer and acceptance. If an offeror confuses the identities of two people and makes his offer to the wrong party, courts frequently try to determine for whom the offer was intended. For example: I make an offer which Marsha Jones accepts. I later protest, on the grounds that I had really meant to make a contract with Marsha Smith, but that I mistook Marsha Jones for Marsha Smith. Now, if it was clear to Marsha Jones that my offer was intended for Marsha Smith, and if her acceptance was made by a letter signed only "Marsha," or by some other method which shows that I had good reason to think I was dealing with Marsha Smith, a court will find that no contract was made. The reason is that my offer was directed solely to Marsha Smith, and that since she never accepted it, there was never valid acceptance, hence never any contract. Suppose, on the other hand, I knew Marsha Smith by sight, and that Marsha Jones accepted the offer in person. In such a case, even though I had previously said my offer was only for Marsha Smith, it is clear that I really intended it to go to Marsha Jones as well, since I received her acceptance without objection, knowing that she was not Marsha Smith.

Some courts have gone further than this. For example: suppose Marsha Jones came to see me and claimed that she was Marsha Smith. Knowing Marsha Smith by reputation, but not by sight, I think highly of her, decide to sell Marsha Jones (who is misrepresenting herself as Marsha Smith) goods on long-term credit. In such a case, some courts would maintain that since I talked with Marsha Jones in person, I had intended the offer for her regardless of what I thought her name was.

As in the prior bicycle example, other factors may be involved. Carelessness is one; if a person makes a mistake because he was negligent, he is likely to lose. The importance of the mistake is another; if it makes very little difference whether I dealt with Marsha Smith or Marsha Jones, a court is much more likely to enforce the contract against me. On the other hand, if Marsha Jones dishonestly leads me to believe that she is Marsha Smith, she will have little chance of winning.

Another way in which courts may consider cases involving contract mistakes does not involve offer-acceptance machinery. They base their decision on the question of which party to the contract had agreed to accept the risk of loss in the event that the mistake, which is now before the court, did occur. If one party agreed to assume the risk that something was true or did happen, that person cannot later escape the contract by claiming he made a mistake. For example: suppose I sell you a used car, which I believe to be in good working condition, for $300. Two days after it is sold, you discover that it needs expensive transmission repairs. You may try to return the car and get your money back, claiming that since both you and I thought the car was in good working order, we both made a mistake about the condition of the goods sold. In deciding the case, a court may say that you can return the car for value because I agreed to take the risk that the car was defective. On the other hand, a court may decide that you agreed to take the risk, and, therefore, you must keep the car. In deciding who has agreed to assume the responsibility, a court will look at several things:

1. The contract may actually state who takes the risk.

2. The custom of the used car trade may determine who is to take the risk.

3. There may be laws which specify who takes the risk. (Section 2-509 of the Uniform Commercial Code is an example of such a law. It provides that when one person sells goods to another, the seller assumes all risks until he delivers the goods; after delivery the buyer assumes the risks.)

Two more comments may be added about the risk approach to cases involving mistakes. The first is bargaining. Generally speaking, an important consideration of the commercial world is "buying cheap and selling dear." Our society customarily holds that, if a man is smart enough to buy something at a low price and later sell it for more, he ought to be entitled to the profit. If a person is not quite so foresighted or keen and makes a bad bargain, thereby losing money, he shouldn't be able to escape the bargain by claiming that he made a mistake. For this reason, courts look at the "risk." From the point of view of the law, a seller always risks losing money, even though he may believe, at the time of the contract formation, that he made a good bargain. Therefore, the party must bear the kind of loss suffered under a normal risk.

A second important consideration is the nature of the risk. The exact limits of the risk make a great deal of difference in how a case turns out. For example: I contract to sell you a car. Normally, you agree to take the risk that car prices may drop in the future. So, if I sell you the automobile, and car prices go down, you cannot claim mistake, return the car, and get your money back. On the other hand, suppose you and I both believe the car to be an Aston Martin and price it on that basis. After the transaction, you find out that the car is really a Jaguar and worth a great deal less than the amount you paid. In such a case, you would be able to return the car and get your money back. While you had assumed the risk of a change in the *market* price of cars, you did not take on the risk of a reduction in worth due to the difference in value between the two automobiles.

One-Sided Mistakes

It is often said that a *one-sided mistake*—that is, a mistake which is made solely by one party—will have very different legal results than a mutual mistake made by both parties to a contract. This is to some extent true, but whether or not the mistake is one-sided is only one factor among many to be considered. In the preceding subsection, we saw that carelessness and the importance of the mistake were factors which also affected the legal outcome.

In discussing one-sided mistakes, we shall examine the effects of one-sided mistakes in general, then look at a common kind of one-sided mistake and the findings courts have reached in such cases in the past.

A one-sided mistake greatly influences the remedy a court will apply. This is best seen in the previous example in which I offer to sell you a "bike" (meaning a dilapidated bicycle) for $50, and you, thinking that you will get a new racing bike, accept my offer. Both people have made a mistake, since each misunderstood the other. In this situation, there are several things a court may do: (1) it may declare that there is no contract; (2) it may decide to enforce the contract according to your interpretation, or (3) it may decide to enforce the contract according to my meaning. The court's decision will depend on the factors discussed earlier; that is, whether the mistake is important enough to cause hardship to either party if the contract is cancelled or enforced, and whether carelessness played a part in the misunderstanding. At any rate, the court will consider all three possible solutions for settling the dispute and will choose the one which it thinks to be the most fair.

Now, suppose that I made this offer while standing in my bicycle shop, pointing to the old bike. Under these circumstances, the mistake would be solely yours, a one-sided mistake, and the effect of this mistake is to reduce the number of possible solutions. A court will not even consider enforcing the contract according to your meaning, but will consider only whether to enforce the contract according to my meaning, or whether to void the agreement. Even if the court decides to cancel the contract, it will do so in a particular manner. In the case of a two-sided mistake, a court is likely to simply cancel the contract, dissolving all duties and performances without damages. In effect, the court says that a contract never existed. When a contract is cancelled because of a one-sided mistake, the court is likely to rule that you must pay me for the loss I suffered in the process of making the contract. Thus, the court may award me compensation for the time and labor I spent on the sale, or for the difference between the sale price to you and that which I actually received from a later buyer. The contract may be cancelled because of your mistake only if I can regain the position I had before I made the contract with you. If it turns out that my previous position cannot be regained the court will usually refuse to cancel the contract.

Another important consideration regarding one-sided mistakes is to determine how one-sided they are. Suppose, in the last example, that as I stood in my bicycle shop, I intentionally offered to sell you an ordinary bicycle, knowing that you were looking for a racing bicycle. Although you have still made a mistake, I was partly responsible because, knowing your intent, I could easily have cleared up the misunderstanding. In such a case, a court is likely to be much easier on you when deciding the dispute. The effect of a one-sided mistake in any given case, therefore, depends on how one-sided the mistake is and on how easily the person who did not make the mistake can recover the position he had before the contract was made.

Now we may proceed to look at the most common kind of one-sided mistake. This results when one person makes an error in figuring a bid, or in computing the price he is going to charge for goods or services. For example: suppose that you ask me to estimate the cost of building a garage for you. After adding up the cost of the materials and the labor, and figuring a profit margin, we form a contract based on the price terms I have

quoted. Later, however, I find that I've made an error in calcu-
lating my costs—in adding, or perhaps by excluding the cost of
some materials. I have made, quite obviously, a one-sided mistake, a very common one indeed.

Some courts do not allow this kind of mistake to affect the
contract, regardless of its size. I cannot get out of the contract.
Other courts sometimes allow the contract to be cancelled, if the
mistake is so important that I would suffer a great loss if forced
to go through with the contract. In addition, to allow cancellation it must be possible for you to regain the position you had
before you made the contract. If, for example, you had bought
a car and hired someone else to build a driveway to your garage, and if you did these things because you had ordered me to
build the garage, it would be impossible for you to regain the
position you were in before you made the contract with me. In
such a case, a court would not cancel the agreement, although, as
we shall see, it may change its terms. A third possibility is that
you knew of my mistake before you accepted the bid, because
you actually saw the error in my calculations, or else the bid
was so low that it was obvious to you I had made a mistake. In
such a case, a court is likely to cancel the contract.

Mistakes of Law

We have so far been discussing mistakes of fact. In this subsection, we will look at *mistakes of law*, mistakes which occur
when a party does something or refrains from an action on the
erroneous assumption that he has a legal right to so act.

This can be shown easily by an example. Suppose that I make
an oral contract to sell you a bicycle. Suppose also that it is
worth less than the dollar limit in the Sales of Goods section of
the Statute of Frauds. (For more on this, see Chapter 6.) The
contract does not need to be in writing. However, I mistakenly
believe that the Statute of Frauds requires that *all* contracts be
in writing. Therefore, I decide that my contract with you is

unenforceable and sell the bicycle to someone else. When you sue me, I claim that I should be allowed to cancel the contract with you because I made a mistake of law.

In a situation of this kind, courts will not allow me to escape the contract. Many of them say flatly that a mistake of law cannot affect a valid contract.

This general rule is not nearly so rigorous as it purports to be; courts have made quite a few exceptions to it. In cases involving a mistake of law where it is unfair to enforce the contract against the person who made the mistake, courts often find other reasons for cancelling the contract. Courts are gradually changing their ideas with regard to a mistake of law, and someday they will treat a mistake of law in the same way as a mistake of fact.

Impossibility of Performance

General

Sometimes, after a contract is made, it becomes impossible for either of the parties to render performance. We saw examples of such impossibility in our discussion of conditions. Presently, we will examine impossibility from another, broader angle; that is, impossible performances in any contractual situation. Impossibility may be absolute or permanent; for example, in the case where I contract to paint your house and your house burns down.

Impossibility can also be temporary. Suppose I contract to mow your field and before I can begin work, heavy rain floods your land. It is presently impossible for me to mow, but after the water dries up, I will be able to work. In the second subsection, we shall discuss temporary impossibility.

Another type of impossibility occurs when something can be performed, but where changing circumstances make it extremely expensive or difficult. Suppose, for example, that I contract to mow your field, but before I am able to start, a flash flood deposits large quantities of gravel across your land. There is still a field, and, with difficulty, I can plow it. However, because the pebbles may break or dull the blades of the mower, and the grass in the field is largely destroyed, it is neither desirable nor reasonable to mow the field. This is *partial impossibility*, or frustration, and will be discussed in the third subsection.

Finally, we will briefly take up two kinds of impossibility encountered earlier in our discussion of conditions. The first occurs when something happens which defeats the purpose of the contract and makes it senseless—although still technically possible—for either party to go through with the contract. The second kind occurs when it is impossible for one of the parties to perform because the other party has prevented him from so doing. We will discuss these types of impossibility in the last two subsections.

Permanent Impossibilities

A first important point to consider is that permanent impossibility excuses performance only if it is due to an occurrence which precludes *anyone* from rendering that performance. Suppose, for example, that I contract to paint your house; I later go to the racetrack and lose all my money. Without the money to buy paint, it is impossible for me to paint your house; however this circumstance does not excuse me from the obligation, because it is possible for someone else to paint. If your house burns down, however, it is impossible for anyone to paint it. This type of impossibility excuses me. In short, impossibility which arises because of an event which a party has brought upon himself will not excuse performance.

There are several ways in which a performance can become sufficiently impossible, thus excusing it. One is the destruction of the subject of the contract, or through the destruction of something which is necessary to the performance of the contract. The house destroyed by fire is a good example.

There is an important exception to this rule: when a court decides that the person who cannot perform has agreed to take the risk that his performance might become impossible, he is not excused. This exception is similar to the one we encountered in discussing mistakes. Just as a mistake will not excuse a party from a contract when he has assumed the risk of mistake, similarly, impossibility will not excuse him if he has assumed the equivalent risk of impossibility. For example: I contract to sell you my car, but before I transfer it to you, my garage collapses, totally destroying the car. It is impossible for me to perform because the subject of the contract has been destroyed. Nevertheless, I would not be excused from performing, or from compensating you for the loss you suffered because I did not perform, if a court decided that I had assumed the risk that the car might be destroyed. Thus, I would probably have to give you the difference between the price you paid me for the car and the cost of your purchasing one like it from someone else. In order to determine whether I have assumed the risk, a court will consider all the things we mentioned in talking about risk in the section on mistake: the words of the contract; the actions of the parties; the customs of the trade; and the applicable laws, if any.

One more thing should be noted in this connection: only where the subject matter destroyed is unique, will impossibility excuse performance. Thus, if the destroyed subject of the contract is obtainable in the open market, its destruction will not excuse performance, since one may perform simply by supplying another object of the same kind. Suppose, for instance, that I contract to sell you my racing bicycle (a custom made model, not for sale anywhere else), and the contract provides that the risk of loss is mine until you actually get the bicycle. After the contract is signed, but before delivery, my garage collapses, destroying the bicycle. Now, the contract here was for the sale of my unique racing bicycle, one specific bicycle and no other.

The destruction of that bicycle excuses me from fulfilling the obligation because there is no way that I or anyone else could perform. (I would, however, have to pay you for damages.) Suppose, instead, that I contracted to sell you an ordinary bicycle. The contract does not provide for any specific bicycle. My garage again collapses, destroying the bicycle I intended to pass to you. I claim that I intended to use this bicycle to perform and that I am therefore excused by impossibility. Since the contract provided for any bicycle, I am not excused and my intentions are irrelevant. There are any number of people who could perform by selling their bicycle to you. I too could perform my obligation by purchasing another bicycle and transferring it to you.

This last set of examples shows why lawyers are so careful about words in making contracts, which often seem to be loaded with technical and difficult language. The result of a contract dispute very often depends upon how precisely the terms, performances, and objects of the contract are spelled out; if phrased in vague and ambiguous language, contracts can give rise to innumerable disputes, the results of which may be quite unpredictable.

Breach of Contract

There are a number of ways in which a contract may be breached. A *breach* is a situation whereby the duty to which a party has obligated himself, according to the contract, is not fulfilled or is unsatisfactorily performed. After a general look at the various kinds of breaches, we shall consider a special type called anticipatory repudiation. (*Anticipatory repudiation* occurs when a party to a contract announces, prior to the due date of the obligation for which he has contracted, that he will not perform.)

First we will take up the various ways in which breach of

contract obligations may be incurred and the legal consequences of each.

Any duty demanded of a party under a contract which is left unperformed or is performed incorrectly breaches the contract. Several degrees of breach exist: A person obligated under a contract may simply state he will not be bound by it and will perform none of its demands; or he may perform part of his duties and then refuse to go further; or one party to the contract, whose cooperation is necessary before the other party can perform, may refuse to cooperate, or may actively hinder the other party from performing.

Some breaches may be so unimportant they do not substantially affect the agreement's execution, while others frustrate the contract completely. The degree of breach is important in law in determining whether the breach is material, minor, or partial. A *material breach* occurs when a party fails to perform to the extent that the other party does not get substantially what he bargained for. To illustrate, suppose you and I make a contract, and I refuse to do something that the contract requires me to do. If I have already done *substantially* what I am supposed to do, the breach may not be material. If, however, the part which I have left undone is important to our bargained exchange, then I have committed a material breach. For example: you and I agree that I am to build a house for you, with certain specifications. I build the house, but install the wrong color shutters. You come to court and refuse to pay me. My breach is only partial, and if I change the shutters, you must pay me. On the other hand, if I build a barn instead of a house or refuse to start building at all, my breach is total, or material, and you will probably be excused from making any payments to me.

In the case of a *material* or *total breach*, the non-breaching party may be excused from any performance under the contract and can usually compel the other party to pay him for any loss he has suffered. Suppose you and I make a contract which states that I am to plow your driveway, and you are to pay me a set fee. I then intentionally and without reason refuse to plow your

driveway after the heaviest snowfall of the winter; this constitutes a material breach. You may be excused from paying me
for any plowing that has already been done, and I may have to
compensate you for any losses you suffered because I did not
perform under the contract.

Where there is only a *partial breach*, the result is different.
Thus, if I plow the driveway but miss a large area each time, I
have committed a partial breach. In the case of my partial
breach, you are not excused from paying me for what I have
done. But you may reduce the amount to reflect my incomplete
performance.

Finally, several rules should be mentioned which regulate
when and how often one may sue a breaching party. These rules
are designed to keep the amount of litigation to a minimum by
requiring that the parties to a contract, whenever possible, settle
all their differences in one lawsuit or the smallest possible
number of suits.

The first rule is that whenever one sues for breach of contract,
he can sue only once on that breach. For example: suppose you
and I have made a contract, and I break it. You sue me, claiming that my breaking the contract caused you a loss of $100.
You win the case, but later on, you realize that my breach injured you more than you had thought—you really had lost $150
because of my infraction. In such a case, you are unable to sue
again. You have already sued on that particular breach, and
anything you did not recover in that suit is lost to you forever.

Suppose that when you first sued, my breach was only partial;
I had merely delayed performance which was not so important
to you that it constituted a material breach. You sued and recovered a small amount of money. Later it becomes apparent
that I will never perform; at this point the violation becomes a
material breach. Despite the later event, you cannot sue me
again to recover more money; however, in this case, you would
be excused from performing your side of the contract. Your
previous suit does not prevent you from doing this; it merely
precludes your suing again to get more money for your loss.

Let us now examine a contract that calls for a series of acts rather than just one; for example, you contracted to cut the grass on my golf course every two weeks during the summer. Under such terms, it is possible for you to breach every two weeks. Suppose you make partial breaches every other week; that is, when you mow, you do only nine-tenths of the course. The first time you do this, I may sue. When you mow incompletely a second time, I may sue again. This, of course, is not the case in a single-performance contract. But in my former suit on a multiple-performance contract, the previous breach does not prevent me from suing again. Suppose instead, that I do not sue after the first breach, but after you breach a second or third time, I sue. In this suit, I must claim all the losses I have suffered for all the previous breaches. If I only claim the loss suffered from the third breach, I cannot later bring another suit for the loss I suffered from the first and second breaches. This rule is intended to require me to consolidate all my previous complaints into one suit, so that they can all be settled at once. If I fail to do so, I am penalized by being prohibited from ever suing on the previous grievances.

In the example cited, suppose that you had not mowed at all for the first two weeks. Such a violation might well be considered a material breach of the whole contract since, in making the agreement, I bargained for a golf course that would be trim and usable all summer long. The very first breach prevented me from having a neat course, and by the fourth week, the grass was too high for golf. This situation would result in a court's deciding that I did not get substantially what I bargained for. In other words, a material breach in one installment of a multiple-performance contract might well be construed as a material breach of the whole agreement.

Courts are divided in their opinion on this situation, a minority contending that the first breach is also a material breach of the whole contract. Therefore, any future breaches are merely part of the same infraction. Since only a single breach is involved, I can bring only one suit to recover for the loss caused by this breach. Consequently, if I sue after you refuse to mow the first time, I must claim the total loss that I will suffer from your breach of the whole contract, despite the fact that most of the effect of this infraction will occur in the future and is therefore unforeseeable. If you later breach by refusing to mow the second time, it is part of the same violation, and I cannot sue you again.

The majority of courts take the opposite point of view, maintaining that even though your first infraction may be material to the whole contract, your second breach is really a different breach for the purposes of suing. It is unfair and unrealistic, in this view, to ask me when I sue after the first breach to include my claims for losses which I may or may not suffer from succeeding breaches because I have no way of knowing how many breaches there will be, how extensive they will be, or what my total loss will finally be. Therefore, I can sue every time you breach, and the previous suits will not prevent me from bringing the later ones.

It is important to notice, however, that this position is usually taken by the courts only where the first breach does not strongly indicate that there will be succeeding breaches. Suppose, for example, that two weeks after signing the contract to mow the fairway, you default on the commitment and, furthermore, you make it very clear, either by words or conduct, that you will not mow at any time during the summer. In this case, the breach is clearly in violation of the whole contract, and I know exactly how much mowing you are going to do: none. Therefore, it is no longer unfair to ask me to claim for all of the losses I will suffer under the contract. If I sue once, under these contracts, I cannot sue again later, because this would be a second suit for the same breach.

Anticipatory Repudiation

An *anticipatory repudiation* occurs when a party to a contract refuses to perform on the contract *prior* to the time when any of his performance is due. For example: suppose you and I make a contract in October that I will plow your driveway when it snows. In early November, before it snows, and, therefore, prior to my being obligated to plow, I say that I will not do any shoveling this winter. This is an anticipatory repudiation, and courts consider it a total breach of contract. Strictly speaking, there has not yet been any breach, because I have not failed to do anything required by the contract; I cannot logically breach the contract until it snows and I fail to plow. Nevertheless, in most states, an anticipatory repudiation is considered a breach, and there are good practical reasons for so considering it. In the preceding illustration, for example, if I make it clear that I will not perform, it is foolish to wait until it snows before allowing you to sue. It is more convenient and sensible to allow us to settle our dispute ahead of time, to permit you to sue me for damages (if any), dissolve the contract, hire another man to plow your driveway, and release you from the contract before my failure to perform results in much larger damages.

In order for my anticipatory repudiation to be a breach, however, it must be a definite and unequivocal refusal to comply. A statement such as, "I may not have time to plow when it snows," would not be a sufficient refusal to constitute a breach. Or, if I said, "I'm not sure I am obligated under our contract, because I think you fraudulently got me to sign it," this would not be definite enough to be a breach. I have an honest reason for believing that I should not plow unless it has already been determined that I was not fraudulently drawn into the contract. The agreement, may, in fact, still be good when my complaint is resolved.

A refusal to perform in the future must therefore be very definite if it is to be considered a breach of contract. The refusal need not be in words; some actions indicate a sufficiently definite refusal. If, for example, I moved to Palm Beach shortly after making my contract to plow snow, my conduct would show a definite refusal to shovel, since I could not travel a thousand miles to your house whenever it came time for me to shovel.

Suppose, now, that we have a contract, and that I have completely refused to perform in accordance with the terms of the agreement. This anticipatory refusal is a breach, and once it has occurred, there are a number of options open to you before a court:

1. You may sue me for the loss you will suffer because of my refusal to perform. To do so, however, you must first show the court that you are ready, willing and able to go through with your side of the bargain. For example: if the contract stated that I would paint your house and that you would pay me for it, you must show the court that you are willing and able to pay me for the work if I refuse to do the job.

2. You can treat my refusal as a counter offer and agree to rescind the contract in the manner described earlier in this chapter under discharge.

3. You can wait until my refusal becomes an actual breach. Suppose, for example, that the contract stipulates that I was to paint your house for which you agreed to pay me $100 in advance and $200 when the job was finished in September. When I refuse to paint, you can withhold both the advance and the amount due on completion, at which time you can also sue me for any other damages caused by my breach; for example loss of buyers for the house because of its shabby appearance.

4. Finally you may choose to ignore my refusal and persuade me to change my mind; if I then start painting, however, you cannot sue for breach. For example, suppose I had agreed to paint your house in the summer, but I refuse to do so; you may ignore the refusal and persuade me to change my mind. I have not yet started performance, though, and you may still decide to sue me for breach on my original repudi-

ation of the contract. But if, after changing my mind, I go out and buy brushes, paint, and a ladder, relying on your refusal to honor my breach, you cannot sue for breach.

After first refusing to paint, I may change my mind and perform until you either institute a lawsuit or notify me that you have decided to rescind the contract. In other words, when you choose one of the alternatives open to you, I am bound by your action and can no longer honor the contract and perform.

There is, of course, a problem in determining when you have made your choice. Courts feel that one of several things is enough to indicate that you have made a choice to hold me to a breach and that it is too late for me to change my mind and perform:

1. It is obvious that if you actually bring suit, by filing a complaint in court, you have decided that I cannot perform.

2. If you go to expense or effort, indicating that you have made a choice to accept my breach, I cannot then honor the contract. (For example: if I have contracted to paint your house and subsequently refuse to perform, you may then hire someone else to do the work. Your conduct would be sufficient proof to indicate that you have chosen to rescind the contract with me.

3. Once you notify me of your decision to rescind, it is too late for me to change my mind.

Remedies

The penalty which a court is willing and able to impose upon the loser in a lawsuit to compensate the winner is called a *remedy*. Remedies for breached contracts are of three main types:

1. *Damages,* or money, which must be paid by the loser to the other party.

2. *Specific performance,* meaning that the court orders the loser to carry out his part of the contract.

3. *Restitution,* whereby a court orders the loser to return to

the winner whatever the latter has already given him under the terms of the contract.

We will look at each of these three remedies in turn.

Damages

In their award of money damages to the winning party in a suit, courts face the problem of how much the loser is to pay. The court's aim is primarily to enable the prevailing party to gain the same position he would have had if the contract had been properly carried out. First, then, a court attempts to figure out how much the loser's performance was worth. If the winner has completely performed, that amount goes to him. The court will figure out how much the winner's remaining performance would have cost him, and then deduct that amount from the value of the loser's promised performance, awarding the plaintiff the difference. Suppose, for example, that I contract to sell you a car for $1,000 and I then sell the car to someone else. You sue me and win. In figuring damages, the court first decides what the car is worth. Let us say that it is now worth $1,500. Then, the court will estimate the worth of your promised performance; in this case $1,000. Subtracting the value of the car ($1,000) from the dollar worth of my promised performance ($1,500), a court would award you damages of $500.

If you had already paid me the full contract price of $1,000 for the car, the court would deduct nothing from the value of the car, and I would have to pay you $1,500 in damages.

This process shows how a court usually computes damages. A number of problems may arise, however. First, measuring the value of the loser's performance may be difficult. (In the preceding example, no problem arises since the loser's performance value is simply the car). Second, it is difficult in many cases to figure out how much the winner's performance would be worth. (In the example above, the cost of your performance is obviously $1,000. If, however, your performance was to be that you would paint my house in return for the car, a court would have more difficulty in determining the cost.)

Let us begin by looking at how a court may decide the value of the loser's undone performance. First, the value of that performance (in the last example, a car) may be measured by its value to the winner; that is, what it would cost him to get from someone else, a car exactly like the one promised. So, in the last example, the court would try to figure out how much the car is worth to you, not to me. If it would cost you $1,500 to buy a similar car from someone else, $1,500 is the value of my performance, even though the car was only worth $1,000 to me because I can get cars at wholesale prices. The easiest way to figure out what the car is worth to you is to find out what it would cost you to replace the car you should have received from me. This is frequently the standard which courts use in evaluating replacement value of a performance.

A third consideration about the value of my performance to you requires that the measurement of damages takes into account only the direct consequences of my failure to perform. Usually you could not claim, for instance, that the car was worth $2,000 to you because you had made another contract with Fred to sell it to him for $2,000. This second contract above market price is unexpected and remote, and it would be unfair to make me pay for your loss on the contract with Fred, when I had no way of knowing that my failure to deliver the car would result in such consequences.

If I have reason to know that you will suffer a loss on the contract with Fred, then my failure to deliver will make me liable for your loss. This would be true if you told me when we contracted that you needed the car for resale to Fred at $2,000; my failure to deliver would then make me liable for the larger amount. The deciding factor is whether, at the time I made the contract with you, I should have reasonably predicted that you would lose the extra amount. If I could predict the extra loss, either because you told me or because of knowledge that I gained in some other way, I would have to pay for it. This extra amount is called *consequential damages,* because it results from something which is consequent to my breach, rather than a direct result thereof.

The other side of computing damages is the value of the performance that the winner was required to render. In the car example, this value is easy to estimate, since the cost of your performance is determined by the amount you agreed to pay; that is, the contract price of $1,000. Suppose, however, that the situation is changed and I contract to sell you a car for $1,000. I go to your house with the car, but you refuse to accept it. I sue you and win. In this case, the value of your undone performance is the contract price of $1,000. But what is the cost of my performance? How much should be deducted from the $1,000 to give a true estimate of the amount I lost because you refused to buy? One answer is that the cost to me of my undone performance is what I paid for the car. However, this is not the right answer, for the recovery of that amount would put me in a *better* position than I would have had if you had gone through with the contract. For example, suppose I had bought the car for $500. If you had gone through with the contract, I would have made a profit of $500. If my cost is $500, however, my damages, in line with the answer above, are $500. But I still have the car, and I can sell it to someone else for $800, thus making a total profit of $800 ($500 in damages and $300 profit on the sale of the car for $800). This would be *more* profit than I would have earned had you gone through with your part of the contract.

A court will usually say, instead, that the expense to me of my performance is the amount that I could get if I sold the car to someone else. Thus, I get an amount of damages equal to the contract price to you minus what I can get from a sale to someone else; that is, contract price less market value or present resale value. This amount is a fair measurement since damages equal the profit that I lost through your failure to perform. Suppose, for example, that I contracted to sell you my car for $1,000. It also appears that I could have sold the car to someone else for $800. In that case, I really would have lost $200 by your refusal to take the car (assuming the other buyer is now also unwilling and I am stuck with the automobile). It is difficult to say that $800 is the expense to me of my own performance, because my expense, strictly speaking, is really what I paid for the car, not the price for which I could have sold it. On the other hand, when I sell the car to you, I am giving up something of value which I could have sold to someone else. In this sense, I am giving up an $800 object when I give away the car, and, therefore, one can say that the cost of my performance is $800.

As already mentioned, in determining how much I could have made by selling the car to someone else, a court commonly looks to the market price. If cars of that make and year usually sell for $800, a court will allow me to recover $300. The market price of an object, of course, varies from place to place and over a period of time. Suppose, for example, that I lived in Pickneyville and you lived in Rock Falls. I contracted to sell you a car for $1,000 and to deliver it to Rock Falls on July 1st. After delivering it, however, you refuse to take the car, whereupon I sue and win. The court discovers I could have sold the car for $400 in Pickneyville on July 1st, but in Rock Falls on that date, I could easily have sold it to someone else for $900. Therefore, my damages would be $100, not $600.

This example points out an important principle of damages: when a seller is left with goods on hand because of the buyer's refusal to accept them, the seller must make a reasonable attempt to market them at the best price obtainable. In legal terms, he must *mitigate* his own damages. Going back to the preceding example, the reason for awarding me $100 instead of $600 is that the car was worth $900 to me; that is, its market price at the time and place I was willing to part with it, as stated in the contract. Similarly, if cars are worth $600 in Rock Falls on *June* 1st, and $900 in Rock Falls on *July* 1st, it is the $900 amount which counts. The reason is, once again, that $900 is the value to me of what I would have given up in Rock Falls on July 1st.

Sometimes, however, there may be no market price for an object or, at best, a very unreliable one. Suppose, for example, I contract to sell you a painting by a controversial, unknown, modern artist for $500. When I deliver the painting, you refuse to take it. There is no reliable way of ascertaining how much I could have gotten had I sold the painting to someone else because there is no definite market price for works by this artist. Some people are enthusiastic about his paintings and might pay $1,000 for one of them. Others regard his work as mediocre and would pay very little for them. In such a case, if I sold the painting for the best price I could get, the court would award me the difference between the contract price of $500 and the amount I actually received, if it was less. If the latter price was higher, neither you nor I would be entitled to damages. You are not permitted to benefit because of your wrong-doing.

Sometimes, however, it may simply be impossible to figure out what I could have gotten if I had sold to someone else; that is, there are no willing buyers. It is impossible, therefore, to know the market value of the winner's performance. Alternatively, it may be impossible to compute the value to the winner of the performance he was to receive. In such a case, courts cannot award the winner damages based upon the profit he would have made if the deal had gone through. Therefore, courts award damages in the amount of expenses incurred by the winner, in his performance under the contract. These expenses do not have to benefit the loser. For example, suppose I live in Pickneyville and contract to sell you a car which I agree to deliver to you in Rock Falls. I go up to Rock Falls with the car and you refuse to buy it. I do not sell the car to anyone else, nor do I now wish to. There is no market value for the car. In this example, a court would allow damages in the amount of the cost of transporting myself and the car to Rock Falls, plus any other reasonable expenses incurred in my performance. This is so even though you received no benefit from my ex-

penditures. Damages of this kind are actually a form of restitution, which we will examine later in this section.

Liquidated Damages

Sometimes the parties to a contract insert a clause stating
exactly what damages one or both parties will have to pay if
the contract is breached. These pre-stated damages which the
parties include in the agreement are called *liquidated damages*,
and a court often enforces them. However, if the amount of the
damages specified in the contract is so high as to constitute a
penalty, a court will then ignore the clause and compute damages in the usual way.

The court's decision to enforce a liquidated damages clause
depends on whether the amount is reasonable. If it is dispro-
portionately high or low, the court will call it a penalty, even
though the contract may specifically state that the liquidated
damages are not a penalty. There are several factors which may
indicate that the amount is unreasonable:

1. If the amount shown in the document as damages is clearly
greater than the worth of the performance under the contract,
a court is likely to call it unreasonable and, therefore, a penalty.

2. If the amount is so inadequate—compared to the actual
damages suffered by the injured party—that great injustice
would result, the court may strike the clause and award actual
damages.

3. If the amount stated in the liquidated damages clause is
a single, fixed amount, regardless of whether the breach is
major or minor, partial or total, a court is likely to call it unreasonable. (This third variety is called a "blunderbuss
clause.")

Keeping the Damages Low

The last topic on damages has been hinted at in the preceding
subsection. When one party breaches a contract, the other party

is required by law to keep the damages resulting from the breach as low as possible. This duty does not demand that the non-breaching party go to extremes to keep the damages down, but only that he take reasonable measures to minimize them. A good idea of what this means can be obtained through several examples:

I contract to sell you a car for $2,000; at the time we make the agreement, you tell me that you have a contract with Fred to resell the car for $2,500. I fail to deliver the automobile, and you sue me for breach of contract. If there is a market for the particular make of car at an average price of $2,000 or less, it is reasonable to expect you to buy a similar car elsewhere for resale to Fred, and therefore, you cannot claim the additional $500 in damages for loss of the sale.

On the other hand, if the particular make of automobile can be bought only in England, and Fred will not accept a substitute, you would be entitled to the additional $500 in damages. Similarly if the auto were a custom-made, one-of-a-kind model, and a substitute could not be purchased anywhere in the world, at any price, the court would award you the extra $500 for loss of anticipated gains from the sale, should you desire money damages and not the car itself. Nor would the law require you to buy another car to meet the terms of your contract with Fred.

Suppose that I contract to build a garage for you, and you agree to pay me in monthly installments from the time I begin work. You then break the contract. I am obligated to stop work on the garage when you breach, because I would be increasing the damages unreasonably by spending more on construction. If I do continue work, you are responsible only for the loss I suffered before you broke the contract.

Specific Performance

An alternative remedy to the payment of money damages, in many cases, is *specific performance*. It requires the loser of a lawsuit to convey the specific item or to complete the performance agreed upon in the contract. Specific performance, however, is allowed only when it is clear to the court that money damages will be insufficient or inappropriate to compensate the complainant for what he has lost; for example, if the article bargained for is unique and irreplaceable or has sentimental value. On the other hand, suppose I contract to sell you ten boxes of bobby pins and then I refuse to do so. In such a case, you could not get specific performance because a money payment would adequately compensate you for your loss; that is, you could immediately purchase ten other boxes on the market. Suppose instead that I contract to sell you "Guernica" by Picasso, a painting of which you are especially fond. Since there is only one such painting in the world, if I then refuse to sell it to you, no amount of money can make up for what you failed to get. Therefore, a court would give you specific performance and order me to sell the painting to you.

The most common situation in which specific performance is awarded involves breaches of contract respecting the sale of real estate. Since no two pieces of land are identical, money will not adequately compensate the buyer if the seller refuses to sell. Although money damages will enable the plaintiff to buy another piece of land, the substitute lot will not be exactly the same as the one originally contracted for. Throughout history the law has recognized the absolute right to land once it has been contracted for.

Even if it appears that a complainant is entitled to specific performance, there are two reasons why a court may not make this remedy available. First, specific performance will not be decreed by the court unless the order can be enforced. In the aforementioned example concerning the sale of Picasso's "Guernica," if I refuse to give you the painting, the court can send the sheriff to seize it and deliver it to you.

On the other hand, suppose that a famous artist contracted to paint your portrait; subsequently he refuses to do so. In such a case, damages may not be adequate since you contracted for a portrait created by the painter's personal, unique skill which you cannot buy elsewhere. A court, however, would be reluctant to demand specific performance because it would be impossible to enforce the order. True, it could order the artist to paint the portrait, but there would be no way of ensuring that he would use all of his artistic ability for which you had contracted. The court could put the painter in jail for contempt; however, that is very unlikely. Therefore, the court would not give specific performance.

A second reason why a court may fail to give specific performance is that the remedy would be unfair. Except in the case of contracts for the sale of land, the decision of whether to order specific performance is left completely to the discretion of the court. A court allows this remedy only when it feels that specific performance is equitable, the best, or at least one of the best, solutions to the dispute.

Restitution

Restitution is a remedy which is given when a contract is dissolved by the court, putting the parties in nearly the same positions as they were in before the contract was signed. It occurs when the party who is injured by breach is able to retrieve the value of the performance he has rendered under the contract. The party seeking restitution must be entitled to rescind the contract. We have already seen four examples of situations in which rescision was allowed to the injured parties; that is, circumstances which rendered the contract void.

Where there is a failure to fulfill a condition, or a mistake is made in the formation of a contract; or a material breach occurs, (including an anticipatory repudiation); or performance becomes impossible, rescision is available to the injured party.

In all the situations discussed above, an innocent party was excused from performance when the condition of mistake, or impossibility occurred. But what of the party who has already partially performed at the time he is excused? In such a case, he is entitled to restitution; that is, he can get back the value of what he has already done, or sometimes recover the specific object in question. Remember, however, that a person is entitled to restitution only if he has been excused from the contract on one of the grounds discussed in the preceding section.

If a person is entitled to restitution, he may ask the court for it, but he does not have to elect it. Restitution is an alternative remedy to money damages or specific performance, and it is not mandatory; a person entitled to restitution can choose either damages or specific performance.

In awarding damages, the court tries to put the winner in the position he would have been in *had the loser properly fulfilled the contract*. The idea behind restitution is entirely different; here, the aim of the court is to put the winner in the position he had *before the contract was made*. This may be effected by making the loser give back what he got from the winner or by ordering the defendant to pay the plaintiff for the value of his performance. Three things follow from this:

1. The winner must give back to the loser anything that he received from him under the contract. If the plaintiff does not do so, he is not entitled to restitution.

2. The amount that the winner receives is usually determined by the value of his performance under the contract. The value of the winner's performance to the loser carries little weight; recovery is measured by determining how much the winner would have gotten if another person had paid for his performance.

3. It makes no difference that the value of what the winner did amounts to more than he was to get for the complete job under the contract; he still recovers the value of what he put into the performance, except in very rare cases.

These three points can be illustrated by an example: Suppose I contract to build a garage for you, and you agree to pay me $2,000 for the work in two installments: $1,000 down, and

$1,000 when the job is finished. You make the down payment, and I begin work. I have expended $3,000 worth of materials and labor when you breach the contract. It is a material breach and entitles me to restitution. Seeking restitution, the court tries to restore the position I was in *before* I made the contract; accordingly I must return the $1,000 down payment which you gave me. The amount I receive is determined by what a third person would have paid for my expenditure on materials and labor; that is, the market value of labor and materials used. I will now get $3,000, whereas I would only have gotten $2,000 if the contract had been completed. The value of my performance determines the measure of my recovery.

There is a final situation in which restitution operates under different rules than those described above. Suppose you and I have a contract. I partially fulfill my obligations and then breach the contract. In certain circumstances, if my breach is minor, and I have already fulfilled most of the agreement, the damages caused by my infraction would be much less than the value of what I have already done. In such a case, I can sue for restitution in the amount by which my past performance exceeds the damages caused by my breach. In order to do so, however, I must show that I did not intentionally break the contract, but that my breach was the result of carelessness. Furthermore, the amount of restitution is measured differently. In this situation, the value to a third person of the materials and labor which I have used is irrelevant. The crucial factor is the benefit which you have derived from these expenditures. For example, if I had contracted to build you a garage, I might have spent a lot of money renting bulldozers and hiring men to run them in order to make an excavation. The only benefit you have received, however, is a yawning hole in your lawn.

9. The Uniform Commercial Code

Its Application

THE Uniform Commercial Code is a long statute containing many provisions. It was first drawn up by a committee of eminent members of the legal profession who wanted to create a model statute which would cover most commercial transactions. The organizing committee had hoped that all the states would adopt the code and thus make the different laws throughout the country uniform. Although the code is nothing more than a committee report, a majority of the state legislatures have already passed it into law, and others are doing so every year. Eventually the Uniform Commercial Code will be the law throughout the land, and the objective of the organizing committee will be realized. (The chart at the end of this chapter indicates those states in which the U.C.C. has already become law.)

The Uniform Commercial Code is made up of ten articles:

● Article 1 contains general rules.

● Article 2 covers contracts for the sale of goods.

● Article 3 is concerned with *commercial paper;* that is, checks, bank drafts, etc.

● Article 4 sets up rules regulating bank procedures for collecting checks or drafts.

• Article 5 covers letters of credit.

• Article 6 regulates bulk transfers (the sale by a business-man of most or all of his inventory, usually because of financial difficulty).

• Article 7 deals with warehouse receipts and bills of lading.

• Article 8 covers securities; that is stocks and bonds.

• Article 9 is concerned with secured transactions, such as mortgages, merchandise purchased on time, etc.

• Article 10 contains provisions regarding the effective date and the laws repealed by the code for state legislatures which might adopt the U.C.C.

Each of the articles is divided into parts, and each part into several sections. Each section is designated by four numbers; for example, 2-403: the first digit indicates that this Section is in Article 2; the second numeral means that the Section is in Part 4 of Article 2, and the last two numbers show that the Section is the third in Part 4 of Article 2. Similarly, 2-322 means that this is Section 22 in Part 3 of Article 2.

These numbers vary according to the practice in each state for numbering laws. For example: in California the numbers are run together so that 2-322 becomes 2322. In other states, like Kentucky, a prefix is added so that 2-322 becomes 355.2-322. In still other states, like Alaska, the numbers are completely different. The chart at the end of this chapter shows the method of numbering in each state which has adopted the code. In our discussion, we will use the numbers as they appear in the committee report before they were altered by any state; that is, the numbers just described.

The code covers many other subjects as well as contracts; in fact the only part of the code which relates directly to the subject matter of this book is Article 2, which covers sales. Bear in mind that when we talk about the code, we are referring to contracts for the sale of goods. If the code makes changes in previous contract law, it will obviously affect agreements for the sale of goods. Many times, however, we have discussed other kinds of contracts which are unaffected by the code; for example, contracts for labor, services, marriage, the sale of land, or anything other than the sale of goods.

How the Code Differs From Basic Law

We have already encountered some provisions of the code. In the section discussing the occasions when a written contract is necessary, we dealt with the Statute of Frauds provisions in the code. In Chapter 8, in the section on "Impossibility," we encountered the risk of loss provision of the code. In the section on "Implication," in Chapter 7, we looked at the implied warranties which the code sets up. If you want to check on these code provisions, refer back to these chapters.

Many of the provisions in the code do not change the previous law: basically they are a summary of what the pre-existing law was. The code provision on parol evidence, discussed in Chapter 6, for example, is essentially a codification of previous law.

We will not consider those parts of the code which coincide with previous law. Instead, we will look at the few sections of the code which differ markedly. This being the case, you should remember that we are skipping over most of the code and, consequently, we will not get a completely accurate idea of what happens in every contract for the sale of goods in states where the code has been passed.

The first point of note is that in contracts for the sale of goods, in states which have adopted the code, seals have been completely abolished.

The first important point concerns changes in a contract after it has been made. As we saw in the sections on consideration and discharge, attempts to change a contract and to substitute new duties may be void for lack of consideration. The code, however, alters this. A revision in a contract need not have consideration to be valid. The code does specify, however, that the change must be made in good faith. This means that the parties to a contract can alter it even if there is no consideration for the change, but each of them must act honestly in making the revision.

Another important aspect of the code is that courts are given much greater powers to strike down contracts. Under Section 2-302, they can cancel a contract whenever they feel that it is completely one-sided, unfair, or unjust. Previously, courts could achieve the same result by interpreting the words of the contract in a technical way, or by saying that the contract was contrary to public policy. Under the code, however, judicial bodies are encouraged to rescind unfair contracts, and they may do so more often.

The code also has a series of provisions dealing with ambiguities in the terms of contract. As we saw in the chapter on Offer and Acceptance, courts will often annul a contract which is so unclear that there has been no meeting of minds. The provisions of the code, generally speaking, make it less likely that a court will rescind a contract for being too indefinite. In doing so, the code gives courts wide powers to clarify ambiguous terms, and puts great weight on making these added terms "commercially reasonable;" that is, reasonable according to the business practices in the particular kind of industry involved.

One major difference between the code and previous law lies in the framework the U.C.C. has developed to control contract performance. This framework can be briefly described as follows: The seller is not entitled to be paid until he has delivered the goods, or has offered to deliver them. In this sense, it can be said that the code makes delivery a constructive condition which must be fulfilled before payment is made.

When the seller delivers the goods, or offers to do so, the buyer has a right to inspect them. He need not accept them if they are in any way damaged, defective, or different from that which was specified in the contract. If the buyer rejects the merchandise, he must either give it back to the seller or hold it until the seller comes to take it back. Under special circumstances, he is entitled to sell the goods, provided he gives the money he receives to the seller.

If the buyer accepts the goods, however, he is bound to keep them, unless they are *materially impaired;* that is, their value greatly reduced because of defects which the buyer could not have discovered before he accepted them.

Another difference between the code and previous law is in the area of "impossibility." In our discussion of impossibility, we saw that courts were not likely to excuse performance just because it was expensive or difficult. They would generally require the performance to be actually impossible; however under the code, this is changed. A person is excused from performing whenever unpredictable events occur which make his performance "commercially impractical." Therefore, under the code, a performance does not have to be actually impossible; it only needs to be impractical.

A final difference between the code and pre-existing law is the manner in which remedies are handled. Under previous law, the winner of a lawsuit had three alternatives: damages; specific performance; or restitution. Under the code, remedies are granted much more liberally and a complainant can be awarded all of these remedies if necessary, instead of having to choose between them. A court will pick out remedies and give them in whatever combination it feels is most fair.

The remedies themselves depend on the framework for performance which we described earlier. Thus, the seller can get remedies if the buyer wrongfully refuses to accept the goods, or if the buyer wrongfully takes back his acceptance. The buyer can obtain remedies if he rightfully refuses to accept or rightfully takes back his acceptance. In addition, remedies are granted for failure to pay for goods, for repudiation, or for failure to deliver goods.

A final difference regarding remedies concerns resale, on which the code puts great emphasis. If the buyer refuses to take goods, the seller must sell them to someone else before he can get damages. His damages are then the difference between what he would have gotten under the contract and what he did get when he sold them to someone else.

If a buyer receives defective goods and rightfully refuses to accept them, he can resell them and deduct the damages he has suffered from the amount he receives.

States in Which the Code Is in Force

Note: This information is taken from
Brancher and Sutherland, *Commercial Transactions:*
Selected Statutes, 1964, p. ix.

State	When Code Became Effective	Method of Numbering Code Sections
Alabama	1/1/67	Code of Alabama, Title 7A, Sections 1-101—10-104
Alaska	1/1/63	Statutes, Sections 45.05.002 —45.05.794
Arizona	1/1/68	A.R.S. Sections 44-2201—44-3202
Arkansas	1/1/62	Statutes 1947, Sections 85-1-101—85-9-507
California	1/1/65	Commercial Code Sections 1101-10104
Colorado	7/1/66	Revised Statutes, Sections 155-1-101—155-11-102
Connecticut	10/1/61	General Statutes, Revision of 1958, Sections 42a-1-101—42a-9-507
Delaware	7/1/67	55 Delaware Laws, Ch. 349, Sections 1-101—10-101
District of Columbia	1/1/65	D.C. Code, Sections 28:1-101 et. seq.
Florida	1/1/67	F.S.A. Sections 671.1-101—680.10-105

State	When Code Became Effective	Method of Numbering Code Sections
Georgia	1/1/64	Code, Title 109A, Sections 1-101—10-106
Hawaii	1/1/67	Laws of 1965 No. 208
Idaho	1/1/68	Idaho Code, Sections 28-1-101 et. seq.
Illinois	7/2/62	Revised Statutes 1961, Chap. 26, Sections 1-101—9-507
Indiana	7/1/64	Burns Statutes Annotated, Sections 19-1-101—19-9-507
Iowa	7/4/66	I.C.A. Sections 554.1101—554.10104
Kansas	1/1/66	K.S.A., Sections 84-1-101—84-10-104
Kentucky	7/2/60	Revised Statutes, Sections 355.1-101—355.9-507
Maine	12/31/64	Revised Statutes, Chap. 190, Sections 1-101—9-507
Maryland	2/1/64	Annotated Code, Article 95A, Sections 1-101—9-507
Massachusetts	10/1/58	General Laws 1932, Chap. 106, Sections 1-101—9-507
Michigan	1/1/64	Compiled Laws 1948, Sections 440.1101—440.9994
Minnesota	7/1/66	M.S.A., Sections 336.1—101—336.10—105

State	When Code Became Effective	Method of Numbering Code Sections
Mississippi	4/1/68	Code 1942 Sections 1-101—10-105
Missouri	7/1/65	Revised Statutes, Mo. 400.1-101—400.10-102
Montana	1/1/65	Revised Code 1947, Sections 87A-1-101—87A-10-103
Nevada	3/1/67	N.R.S. 104.1101—104.9507
New Hampshire	7/1/61	Revised Statutes Annotated 1955, Sections 382A:1-101—382A:9-507
New Jersey	1/1/63	Revised Statutes 1937, Cum. Supp. Sections 12A:1-101—12A:9-507
New Mexico	1/1/62	Statutes Annotated 1953, Sections 50A-1-101—50A-9-507
New York	9/27/64	Consolidated Laws, Chap. 38, Sections 1-101—10-105
North Carolina	7/1/67	G.S. Section 25-1-101—25-10-107
North Dakota	7/1/66	N.D.C.C. 41-01-02—41-09-53
Ohio	7/1/62	Revised Code, Sections 10301.01—1309.50
Oklahoma	1/1/63	Statutes, 1961, Title 12A Sections 1-101—10-104
Oregon	9/1/63	Revised Statutes, Sections 71.1010—79.5070

Pennsylvania	7/1/54	Purdon's Title 12A, Sections 1-101—9-507
Rhode Island	1/2/62	General Laws 1956, Sections 6A-1-101—6A-9-507
South Carolina	1/1/68	Code 1962 Title 10.1—10.10
South Dakota	7/1/67	S.D.C. 1960 Supp. 1-101—10-102
Tennessee	7/1/64	T.C.A. Title 47
Texas	7/1/66	V.T.C.A. Bus. & C. Sections 1.101—9.507
Utah	1/1/66	U.C.A. 1953 70A-1-101—70A-10-104
Vermont	1/1/67	9A V.S.A. Sections 1-101—9-507
Virginia	1/1/66	Code 1950 Sections 8.1-101—8.10-104
Washington	7/1/67	R.C.W.A. Sections 62 A.1-101—62 A. 10-104
West Virginia	7/1/64	Code Supplement 1963, 46-1-101—46-10-204
Wisconsin	7/1/65	Statutes, Sections 401.101—409.507
Wyoming	1/2/62	Statutes 1957, Sections 40A-10101—40A-9-604

Appendix I

Examples of Contracts

In this section you will find examples of several different kinds of contracts; since their variety is nearly infinite, we have included examples of only the most common ones. These should help make you aware of the obligations each one imposes on the contracting parties. The following examples are included:

Simple Employment Contract

_____(NAME)_____ , the employer, hereby employs
_____(NAME)_____ , the employee, to perform
duties below named, in consideration for which the employer will pay
the employee at the rate of _____ dollars per _____
and, in addition, compensate him for any other expenses incurred by
him in the carrying out of his duties.

In consideration of the above named payments the employee agrees
to carry out the following duties: _____ _____
_____ _____ _____ _____

In all of his work for the employer the employee shall act faithfully,
honestly, and to the best of his ability. At no time shall his performance
fall below the recognized standard for his trade.

This agreement shall take effect on __(DATE)__ __(MONTH)__ , 19____
and continue until __(DATE)__ [Substitute, if desired, "_____ days
after written notice of termination is given by one party to another."]
On the last day of his employment, the employer shall pay all compensation due the employee, and such payment shall be in full satisfaction
of all claims against the employer by the employee under this agreement.

_____(SIGNATURE)_____

Executive Employment Agreement

AGREEMENT, dated as of _____, 19____, by and between _____ (hereinafter referred to as the "Company"), a Massachusetts corporation, and _____ (hereinafter referred to as the "Employee").

The Company desires to secure the services of the Employee in a general executive capacity, and the Employee is willing to accept such employment upon the terms and conditions set forth in this Agreement.

NOW, THEREFORE, in consideration of the premises and the mutual agreements hereinafter set forth, and of the payments to be made by the Company, and the services to be rendered by the Employee, as hereinafter provided, the parties hereto hereby agree as follows:

1. The Company will and hereby does employ the Employee to serve in a general executive capacity, and the Employee will and hereby does accept employment by the Company to perform such duties and services as may from time to time be assigned or delegated to him by the Board of Directors of the Company (hereinafter referred to as the "Board").

2. For the one-year period commencing on the date first above written, the Company will pay the Employee and thereafter will pay or will cause to be paid to the Employee the sum of _____ per year, in pro rata monthly installments at the end of each month, as full compensation for all rights granted and all services to be performed by the Employee under this Agreement. Such payments will be subject to such deductions as are from time to time required to be made pursuant to law, government regulation, or order, or by agreement with, or consent of, the Employee. Such compensation is subject to annual or more frequent review by the Board and may, in the sole discretion of the Board be increased from time to time.

3. The term of this Agreement will commence on (DATE) and will continue until five years thereafter, provided, however, that the obligation of the Company to pay the compensation provided in Section 2 hereof will terminate immediately upon either the total disability or the death of the Employee. As used herein the term "total disability" shall mean the inability of the Employee to perform his normal duties as certified to by a licensed physician chosen by the Company.

4. The Employee will, in the course of his employment, have access to the methods of conducting the Company's business including, without limiting the generality of the foregoing, its methods of obtaining customers, customer lists, and other confidential information. The Employee's position as an executive places him in a position of trust and

confidence with respect to the business of the Company. For the fore-going reasons the Employee will

    (a) faithfully and diligently do and perform such acts and duties in connection with his employment hereunder as may be specified and required by the Board;

    (b) neither directly, or indirectly, own, manage, operate, control, be employed by or connected in any manner with the ownership, management or control of any business, or venture, competing with the business now or hereafter conducted by the Company and its subsidiaries;

    (c) not engage in any other activity which is or may be contrary to the welfare, interest, or benefit of the business now or hereafter conducted by the Company or its subsidiaries; and

    (d) nor at any time in the future, directly or indirectly, disclose or furnish to any other person, firm or corporation, the methods of conducting the business of the Company or any of its subsidiaries; furnish to any person, firm, or corporation a description of any of the methods of obtaining business, of promoting, marketing, or advertising products; or of obtaining customers therefor, and/or disclose to any person, firm or corporation any confidential information acquired by him during the course of his employment by the Company or any of its subsidiaries.

    5. (a) As between the Employee and the Company or any subsidiary all ideas, creations, and properties, whether or not furnished by the Employee and whether or not conceived, and/or developed during regular working hours, created, developed, or used in connection with the Company's business, will be the sole and absolute property of the Company or any of its subsidiaries for any and all purposes whatever in perpetuity. The Employee will not have, and will not claim to have, under this Agreement or otherwise, any right, title or interest of any kind or nature whatsoever in or to any such ideas, creations, and properties.

    (b) All ideas, creations, and properties furnished by the Employee to the Company or any of its subsidiaries will be the Employer's own and original creation except for materials in the public domain and will not to the best of his knowledge or belief violate or infringe upon any right, copyright, trademark or right of privacy, or constitute libel or slander against or violate any other rights of any person, firm, or corporation.

    6. The Employee will, at any time during his employment or after its termination, at the Company's request and without charge to the

Company, but at the Company's expense, sign all requests for assignments or documents of any nature and do any other acts that may at any time reasonably be deemed necessary by the Company to vest in the Company the entire right, title and interest (or as much thereof as is possible in the circumstances) in and to the items referred to in Section 5.

7. The Employee will also, at the request and expense of the Company, assist the Company by testifying:

(a) in any proceeding in which the Company is or may be concerned with respect to the items referred to in Section 5, or any one or more of such items, including, without limitation, any copyright infringement, or other copyright litigation; and

(b) in any other litigation or proceeding in which the Company is or may be concerned involving any matter in respect of which the Employee has any information or knowledge, whether or not related to the items referred to in Section 5.

8. Upon the termination of his employment under this Agreement, the Employee will deliver to the Company any property of the Company which may be in the Employee's possession, including materials, memoranda, notes, records, reports, or other documents.

9. If the Employee should fail or refuse to perform his obligations hereunder, the Company may, in addition to such other rights as it may have, terminate its obligations hereunder forthwith and without notice and without prejudice to any right the Company or any of its subsidiaries has or may have hereunder with respect to securing performance by the Employee of his obligations under Sections 4, 5, 6, 7, 8, 10 and 11 hereof.

10. The parties hereto recognize that immediate and irreparable damage will result to the Company and its subsidiaries, their businesses and properties, if the Employee fails or refuses to perform his obligations under this Agreement and, notwithstanding any election by the Company or any of its subsidiaries to claim damages from the Employee as a result of any such failure or refusal, the Company may, in addition to any other remedies and damages available, obtain an injunction in a court of competent jurisdiction to restrain any such failure or may specifically compel performance by the Employee of his obligations under Sections 4, 5, 6, 7, 8, 10 and 11 hereof. The Employee represents and warrants that in the event of the termination of his employment as herein provided, his experiences and capacities are such that he can obtain employment in business engaged in other lines and/or of a different nature, and that the specific enforcement of the provisions of this Agreement will not prevent him from earning a livelihood.

11. The Employee will execute and deliver all such other and further instruments and documents as may be necessary, in the opinion of the Company, to carry out the purposes of this Agreement, or to confirm, assign or convey to the Company or any of its subsidiaries any ideas, creations, manuscripts, proofs or properties reformed to in Subsection (a) of Section 5 hereof.

12. All notices hereunder shall be in writing and will be deemed to have been given if delivered personally or mailed by registered or certified mail, return receipt requested, postage prepaid, addressed as respectively indicated or to such other address as shall be indicated by a notice hereunder:

    (a) if to the Employee, addressed to him at: _____

_____

    with a copy to his counsel, at _____

_____

    (b) If to the Company, addressed to it at: _____

_____

    with a copy to its counsel, _____

_____

13. Any provision or provisions hereof found to be prohibited by law will be ineffective only to the extent of such prohibition and will not invalidate any other provision of this Agreement.

14. This Agreement will bind the heirs, executors, administrators, successors and assigns of the Employee, and the duly authorized legal representative of the Employee will, upon request of the Company, sign any and all documents reasonably necessary to carry out the purposes of this Agreement including, without limitation, any and all applications for copyright registration and assignments thereof necessary to vest in the Company title to any copyright which Employee is required to assign to the Company by the terms of this Agreement. This Agreement will also bind, and inure to the benefit of, any successor to the business of the Company (including any company to which all of the assets and business of the Company is assigned) provided such successor is an affiliate of the Company.

IN WITNESS WHEREOF, the parties hereto have executed this Agreement as of the date first hereinabove written.

Attest:

                              By_____ (EMPLOYER) _____

(EMPLOYEE)

_____   _____(L. S.)

Contract of Sale of Goods

_____(DATE)_____

Seller:
_____(NAME)_____ of ____(CITY, COUNTY, STATE)__

Buyer:
_____(NAME)_____ of ____(CITY, COUNTY, STATE)__

The seller hereby agrees, in consideration of the promises below, made by the buyer, to deliver to the buyer the following goods: _____(DESCRIBE IN DETAIL)__ _____ on _(DATE OF DELIVERY)__

The buyer hereby agrees in consideration of the above promise of the seller that the buyer shall pay _____ dollars to the seller on ___(DATE ON WHICH PAYMENT IS TO ME MADE)___ .

Seller: _____(SIGNATURE)_____

Buyer: _____(SIGNATURE)_____

General Bill of Sale

Used to transfer title of goods or property.

I, _____(NAME)_____ , of ____(CITY, COUNTY, STATE)__ hereby acknowledge that I am the owner of the following goods: _____(DESCRIBE IN DETAIL)_____ and that they are free from any encumbrances, and that I am free to sell them.

In consideration of _____ dollars received by me from_____(NAME)_____ , I hereby grant delivery and transfer of these goods to_____(NAME)_____ .

These goods shall be the property of _____(NAME)_____ for his own use forever.

Date:
_____(SIGNATURE)_____

General Release

To whom it may concern:

I, _____(NAME)_____ , for and in consideration
of _____ dollars, paid to me by_____(NAME)_____ ,
do release him, his heirs, executors, and administrators, from all claims,
actions and causes of actions of every kind that I have or may have by
reason of any incident, occurrence, or cause from the beginning of the
world to this day.

Dated: _____, 19____.

_____(SIGNATURE)_____

Note: The above is a general release which would cover most situations.
however, for unique circumstances one should use a more specialized
instrument.

General Assignment

Transfers to a third party, claims which were originally due from a
second party.

In consideration of _____ dollars, I, _____(NAME)_____
_____ , hereby assign and transfer to_____(NAME)_____
all rights and interest that I have or would have in the attached contract
between_____(NAME)_____ and me, subject to all its
conditions and terms, and in so doing release and quit claim to all rights
that I have or would have to receive property under that contract.

Date:

_____(SIGNATURE)_____

_____(NAME)_____ hereby accepts this assignment.

Date:

_____(SIGNATURE)_____

Composition Agreement

Used to settle claims of debt.

WHEREAS_____(NAME OF DEBTOR)____, to be referred to as debtor,
cannot meet his payments to us, his creditors, ____(NAME)____; and
WHEREAS we, the creditors, have agreed to accept _____ cents on
the dollar in full satisfaction of his debt to each and every one of us;
THEREFORE, we promise and agree for ourselves, respectively and
severally, and for our successors, heirs and assigns, to accept from
debtor in any claim we have against him _____ cents on the
dollar to be paid as follows:
[set out the manner in which payment
will be rendered to the creditors]
FURTHERMORE, we promise not to sue or arrest debtor or confiscate his
possessions for any existing liability, provided that debtor pays as
is above set out and that all creditors accept this composition agreement; provided also that this agreement will neither avoid the right
of said creditors to go against a surety of the debtor, nor their right
to recover any security they may hold for claims against him.
_____(SIGNATURE OF CREDITOR)____

Note: The promise not to sue is what makes this agreement an effective
composition. A promise by debtor to pay some money at an earlier time
may, in some circumstances, also operate as an enforceable composition
arrangement.

Assignment of Savings Bank Deposit

For value received, I, _____(NAME)_____ , hereby assign and transfer to _____(NAME)_____ , his heirs, executors, and assigns all my right, title, and interest to a savings bank deposit held by me in _____(NAME OF BANK)_____ together with all right, title, and interest to my savings account bank book numbered _____, and all moneys, principal, and interest credited to my account.

To complete the transfer, I have delivered to ____(ASSIGNEE)____ the said bank book with a signed blank draft; and I authorize _(ASSIGNEE)_ to enter the amount of the deposit and any interest accrued to date of withdrawal on said draft; and I authorize _____(BANK)_____ to pay _____(ASSIGNEE)_____ his heirs, executors, and assigns said full amount with interest.

_____(SIGNATURE)_____

Option to Purchase Shares of Stock

AGREEMENT dated _____, 1968 by and between
_____ (hereinafter referred to as the
"Optionee"), and _____ (hereinafter
collectively referred to as "Optionors").

WHEREAS, the Optionee desires to acquire an option to purchase
certain of the shares of common stock of _(NAME OF CORPORATION)_
(hereinafter referred to as the "Company") owned by the Optionors;
and

WHEREAS, each Optionor desires to grant the Optionee an option to
acquire certain of his shares;

Now, THEREFORE, in consideration of the premises, the mutual covenants herein set forth, and other good and valuable consideration, the
Optionee and the Optionors hereby agree as follows:

1. (a) Subject to the terms and conditions set forth herein, each
Optionor hereby grants the Optionee or his assigns an option, exercis-
able ___(SPECIFY PERIOD OF TIME)__ from the date of this Agreement
and at any time prior to the expiration of ___(LENGTH OF TIME)____
from the date of such Agreement, to purchase from each such Optionor
that number of shares of the Company's common stock at_(AMOUNT)_
per Share.

(b) The Optionee may elect to exercise this option as to all or any
part of the shares subject thereto, but any partial exercise shall
terminate any and all rights hereunder with respect to the balance of
the shares otherwise subject to the terms of this Agreement. The
Optionee will give notice of such exercise to the Optionors and of the
time and place for closing of the purchase, which times will not be less
than 10 days nor more than 30 days after the date of the notice. At the
closing, the Optionor will transfer and deliver the shares, with all
requisite stock transfer tax stamps duly affixed, against payment of the
purchase price by delivery of a certified or official bank check. If for
any reason, any Optionor should fail to transfer and deliver such Shares
at the closing upon tender of payment therefor as herein provided,
such Optionor or Optionors hereby authorize and empower the Company (acting by its then President and Secretary, or either of them) to
make, execute, and deliver any and all assignments, transfers, and
powers of attorney in writing necessary or required for the transfer of
such Shares to the Optionee and to cause such Shares to be transferred
and the certificate or certificates theretofore issued therefor to be
cancelled; and thereafter the rights of the Optionor or Optionors shall

be limited to the right to receive and collect the purchase price hereunder.

2. All notices or communications which may be sent under or by reason of any of the provisions of this Agreement will be in writing and delivered personally or sent by registered mail addressed to the Optionors in care of_____(COMPANY)_____ at its principal place of business in____(CITY)____ and to the Optionee at____(ADDRESS)____or such other addresses as the parties hereto may hereafter designate by notice duly given hereunder. Service of notice given by registered mail shall be complete upon mailing and shall be valid for all purposes of this Agreement notwithstanding death, incapacity or the nonappointment of any administrator, executor, or other personal representative of the addressee or the failure to notify anyone else.

3. In the event that at any time prior to the exercise of this option for all of the Shares, the Company shall pay a stock dividend, split, reclassify, subdivide, combine, reclassify, or reduce the Shares of its common stock, the Optionee shall have the right to purchase the number of Shares into which the number of Shares then purchasable hereunder shall be converted or exchanged or transferred by reason of such stock dividend split, reclassification, subdivision, combination, or reduction.

4. Upon any merger or consolidation to which the Company is a party, the Optionee shall be entitled to purchase at the purchase price indicated in Paragraph 1 hereof, in lieu of the number of Shares subject to this option, the number and class of shares of stock or other securities which the Optionors received pursuant to the terms of the agreement of merger or consolidation.

5. Each Optionor agrees not to sell, transfer, or otherwise dispose of the Shares subject to the terms of this Agreement unless the transferee of such Shares shall agree in writing to become a party to, and be bound by, the terms of this Agreement.

6. The Certificate or certificates representing the Shares will bear a printed or typewritten legend in the following form:

> This Certificate of Stock is held by the person named on the face thereof, subject to a contract among shareholders dated _____, 1967, providing certain restrictions on the sale, transfer, or other disposition thereof, which restrictions expire on _____.

Any certificate issued in connection with a stock split, stock dividend, recapitalization, or any other increase or decrease of the number of issued and outstanding shares of common stock made by the Company subsequent to the date hereof without consideration therefor will be subject to the terms of this Agreement and will bear the same legend as the certificate with respect to which it was issued.

7. This Agreement will inure to the benefit of and bind the parties hereto, their respective heirs, executors, administrators and assigns.

8. This Agreement will in all respects be construed under and governed by the laws of the State of ____(WHERE COMPANY IS LOCATED)____ .

9. This Agreement constitutes the entire understanding of the parties hereto and incorporates all prior discussions and agreements between the parties relating hereto.

IN WITNESS WHEREOF, the parties hereto have executed this Option Agreement as of the date first above written.

OPTIONEE:

_____(SIGNATURE)_____

OPTIONORS:

_____

_____

_____

_____

_____

Power of Attorney

Transfers decision-making authority to a second party.

I, _____(NAME)_____ , hereby appoint _____(NAME)_____
my true and lawful attorney for me and authorize him in my name
to demand payment of claims to become due from my _____
business located at _____ and to give releases or dis-
charges for the same, also to perform and execute those things which
he deems necessary to and proper for the carrying on of said business.
_____(SIGNATURE)_____

Note: A power of attorney may spell out more exactly the duties of
management to be assumed by the attorney. These powers are not restricted to the management of business but may also be given for the
management of an estate during the owner's absence or to allow the
attorney to collect monies due in satisfaction of debts to the attorney.

Confession of Judgment

Permits seller to bring judgment against defaulting debtor.

_____ Plaintiff
_____ Defendant

The undersigned confesses judgment in this action in favor of _____ for $_____ and hereby authorizes him, his heirs, distributees, executors, or assigns to enter judgment against the defendant after _____.

This confession of judgment results from a debt to become due to the plaintiff above named, which debt arose from the following transaction:

Note of defendant for $_____ due on _____ given to plaintiff.

The consideration for this sum is _____
_____[SPECIFY LOAN, SERVICE RENDERED ETC.]_____ .

_____ (SIGNATURE) _____

Note: This confession might contain a provision allowing defendant to re-open judgment if the consideration for the debt, which might be an item purchased, turns out to be flawed.

Personal Bond with Surety for Payment of Debt

I, _____(NAME)_____ , as Principal, and _____(NAME OF)_____ Company, as Surety, are firmly bound to _____, its successors and assigns for the sum of $_____ to the payment of which I and Surety bind ourselves, jointly and severally in this agreement.

_____(SIGNATURE)_____

Note: This instrument will also incorporate the arrangement, perhaps a mortgage, out of which the debt has arisen.

Mortgage

The essentials of a valid mortgage are: It must be in writing; The parties thereto must be competent (sane adults); Its purpose must be stated (to secure payment of a specified bond or obligation); There must be an appropriate mortgaging clause ("the mortgagor hereby mortgages to the mortgagee"); The description of the property mortgaged must be stated definitely; It must contain all the mortgagor's covenants prescribed in the statutory short form of mortgage; It must be signed and sealed by the mortgagor; It must be acknowledged by the mortgagor; It must be delivered to the mortgagee.

The statutory short form of mortgage is as follows:

MORTGAGE

This mortgage, made the _____ day of _____ nineteen hundred and _____, between _____ (insert residence), the mortgagor, and _____ (insert residence), the mortgagee.

Witnesseth, that to secure the payment of an indebtedness in the sum of _____ dollars, lawful money of the United States to be paid on the _____ day of _____ nineteen hundred and _____, with interest thereon to be computed from _____, at the rate of _____ per centum per annum, and to be paid _____, according to a certain bond of obligation bearing even date herewith, the mortgagor hereby mortgages to the mortgagee (description).

And the mortgagor covenants with the mortgagee as follows:

1. That the mortgagor will pay the indebtedness as hereinbefore provided.

2. That the mortgagor will keep buildings on the premises insured against loss by fire for the benefit of the mortgagee.

3. That no building on the premises shall be removed or demolished without the consent of the mortgagee.

4. That the whole of said principal sum shall become due after default in the payment of any installment of principal or of interest for _____ days, or after default in the payment of any tax, water rate or assessment for _____ days after notice and demand.

5. That the holder of this mortgage, in any action to foreclose it, shall be entitled to the appointment of a receiver.

6. That the mortgagor will pay all taxes, assessments or water rates, and in default thereof, the mortgagee may pay the same.

7. That the mortgagor within _____ days upon request in person or within _____ days upon request by mail will furnish a statement of the amount due on this mortgage.

8. That notice and demand or request may be in writing and may be served in person or by mail.

9. That the mortgagor warrants the title to the premises.

In witness whereof this mortgage has been duly executed by the mortgagor.

In presence of:

_____   (SIGNATURE OF MORTGAGOR)   (Seal)
                                   (Acknowledgment)

Acknowledgments

Technically, the term *acknowledgment* means both the act and the evidence thereof made by the officer taking the acknowledgment. Practically, an acknowledgment is the certificate of an officer, duly empowered to take an acknowledgment or proof of the conveyance of real property, that on a specified date "before me came _____, to me known to be the individual described in, and who executed the foregoing instrument and acknowledged that he executed the same."

Some forms of acknowledgments are as follows:

By An Individual

STATE of _____,)

County of _____,)

ss.: _____

On this _____ day of _____, before me came _____, to me known to be the individual described in, and who executed the foregoing instrument, and acknowledged that he executed the same.

_____
Notary Public
_____ County, No. _____

By A Corporation

STATE of _____,)

County of _____,)

ss.: _____

On this _____ day of _____, in the year _____, before me came _____, to me known, who, being by me duly sworn, did depose and say that he resides in _____, that he is the _____ of the _____ corporation described in and which executed the above instrument; that he knows the seal of said corporation; that the seal affixed to said instrument is such corporate seal; that it was so affixed by order of the board of directors of said corporation, and that he signed his name thereto by like order.

_____
Notary Public
_____ County, No. _____

Contract For the Sale of Real Property

AGREEMENT, made this _____ day of _____,
19____, between _____ hereinafter
described as the Seller, and _____ hereinafter described as the Purchaser,

Witnesseth, that the Seller agrees to sell and convey, and the Purchaser agrees to purchase all that lot or parcel of land, with the buildings and improvements thereon,

Description; Survey; Restrictions; Leases

The price is _____.

DOLLARS, payable as follows: _____,

DOLLARS on the signing of this contract, the receipt of which is hereby
acknowledged;

DOLLARS on the delivery of the deed as hereinafter provided, either
in cash or by check drawn to the order of the Seller upon a bank which
is a member_____(CITY)_____ Clearing House, and duly certified by
such bank.

DOLLARS by taking said premises subject to a mortgage, now a recorded lien thereon, upon which there is unpaid that principal amount,
which bears interest at the rate of _____ per centum
per annum, the principal of which will become due as follows:

DOLLARS by the Purchaser _____ making,
executing and delivering a purchase money bond and second mortgage
covering said premises, for that amount of principal sum, payable

Such bond and mortgage shall bear interest at _____
per centum per annum, payable _____ yearly. They shall
be drawn upon forms usually employed by one of the Title Companies
of the City of _____ for second mortgages, and the expense of
drawing and recording the same, the mortgage tax thereon and the cost
of the stamps on the bond* shall be paid by the Purchaser at the time
of the execution thereof.

All notes or notices of violation of law or municipal ordinances,
orders or requirements noted in or issued by any Department of the
City or State of _____, against or affecting the premises at the date
hereof, shall be complied with by the Seller and the premises shall be
conveyed free of the same, and this provision shall survive the delivery
of the deed hereunder. The Seller shall furnish the Purchaser with an
authorization to make the necessary searches for such notes or notices.

This sale is made subject to the resolution or ordinance of the Board
of Estimate and Apportionment commonly known as the "Zoning"

Ordinance, and to all amendments thereof and supplements thereto now in force; and also subject to encroachments, if any, of stoops, areas and cellar steps upon any street or highway.

If at the time of the delivery of the deed the premises or any part thereof shall be or shall have been affected by any assessment or assessments which are or may become payable in annual installments of which the first installment is then due or has been paid, then for the purposes of this contract all the unpaid installments of any such assessment, including those which are to become due and payable after the delivery of the deed, shall be deemed to be due and payable and to be liens upon the premises affected thereby and shall be paid and discharged by the Seller, upon the delivery of the deed.

This sale includes all of the right, title and interest of the Seller of, in and to any strips or gores of land adjacent to said premises, and of, in and to any land lying in the bed of any street, road or avenue, open or proposed, in front or of adjoining said premises, to the centre line thereof, and all right, title and interest of the Seller in and to any award made or to be made in lieu thereof, and in any award for damage to said premises by reason of change of grade of any street; and the Seller will execute and deliver to the Purchaser, on closing of title, or thereafter, all proper instruments for the conveyance of such title and the assignment and collection of any such award.

The Seller shall, upon receipt of the price, paid in the manner above stated, make, execute and deliver or cause to be made, executed and delivered a good and sufficient deed to convey to the Purchaser or the Purchaser's assigns, the fee of said premises free from all encumbrances except as herein stated. Such deed shall be delivered at the office of _____ in the Borough of _____ of the city of _____, on _____, 19____, at _____ o'clock ____ M.

All instruments to be given hereunder are to be in the statutory short form except as herein otherwise provided.

---

* Federal tax thereon has been repealed in case of individuals but applies to corporations.

Appendix II

Glossary of Legal Terms

ACCORD AND SATISFACTION: A settlement of a claim whereby the creditor accepts substitute performance in payment of the claim, and the debtor completes such performance. The term may also apply where the creditor agrees to accept substitute performance, and the debtor promises such performance.

AGENCY: That relationship between principal and agent which arises out of a contract, either express or implied, written or oral, wherein an agent is employed by a person to do certain acts on his behalf in dealing with a third party.

AGENT: One who undertakes to transact some business or to manage some affair for another by authority of the other.

AGREEMENT OF SALE: A written agreement between seller and purchaser in which the purchaser agrees to buy certain real estate and the seller agrees to sell upon terms and conditions set forth therein.

ASSET: Anything of value owned by a person, firm, association, or estate which is available for, or subject to, the payment of debts.

ASSIGNEE: The person to whom an agreement or contract is assigned.

ASSIGNMENT: The method or manner by which a right, a specialty, or a contract is assigned from one person to another.

ASSIGNOR: A party who assigns or transfers an agreement or contract to another.

AVOID: To end or cancel something, such as an agreement or contract.

BAILMENT: A transaction in which personal property is delivered by its owner (the bailor) to a second party (the bailee) into whose possession it is put for safekeeping or for some temporary purpose with no intention that title shall pass to the second party.

BENEFICIARY: The person who receives or is to receive the benefits resulting from certain acts.

BILATERAL CONTRACT: A contract formed by an exchange of promises among the parties.

BILL OF SALE: A written instrument given to pass title of personal property from vendor to vendee.

BONA FIDE: In good faith, without fraud, as with a bona fide purchaser.

CHATTEL: Personal property, such as household goods or fixtures.

CONDITIONAL SALES CONTRACT: A contract for the sale of property or chattels stating that delivery is to be made to the buyer, title to remain vested in the seller until the conditions of the contract have been fulfilled.

CONSIDERATION: Anything of value given to induce entrance into a contract; it may be money, personal services, forbearance to do certain things, or even love and affection.

CONTRACT: An agreement between competent parties to do or not to do certain things for a legal consideration, whereby each party acquires a right to certain specified property or goods that the other possesses.

COVENANTS: Agreements written into deeds, leases, and other instruments promising performance or nonperformance of certain acts, or stipulating certain uses or nonuses of the property.

CREDIT: A claim for money or money's worth which is enforceable at law, whether the claim is due or accruing and whether secured or not; e.g., accounts receivable, notes, bonds, accrued interest and rent, bank deposits but not corporate stock.

DAMAGES: The indemnity recoverable by a person who has sustained an injury, either in his person, property, or relative rights, through the act or default of another.

DECEDENT: One who is dead.

DEFAULT: Failure to fulfill a duty or promise, or to discharge an obligation; omission or failure to perform any acts.

DURESS: Unlawful constraint exercised upon a person whereby he is forced to do some act against his will. Contracts made under duress will not be enforced.

EARNEST MONEY: Down payment made by a purchaser of real or personal property as evidence of good faith.

EASEMENT: A right that may be exercised by the public or individuals on, over, or through the lands of others.

ENCUMBRANCE: Any right to or interest in land or chattels, such as a mortgage, which diminishes their value.

EQUITY: Broadly, any interest which will receive recognition and enforcement in a court of equity, whether or not such interest constitutes legal ownership. Specifically, the interest, usually expressed in money's worth, of the equitable owner of a property over and above all liens (q.v.) against the property.

ESCROW: A written agreement between two or more parties requiring that certain instruments or property be placed with a third party to be delivered to a designated person upon the fulfillment or performance of some act or condition.

ESTOPPEL: A legal doctrine barring a party's denying facts which he had previously represented as true, when another person has relied on the representation and has been damaged by such reliance.

EXECUTORY CONTRACT: A contract which has not yet been performed by any of the parties thereto.

EXTINGUISH: To extinguish a debt, to cancel or eliminate the condition of debt.

FEE, FEE SIMPLE, FEE ABSOLUTE: Absolute ownership of real property; a person has this type of estate where he is entitled to the entire property with unconditional power of disposition during his life and through his will.

FIDUCIARY: A person who on behalf of or for the benefit of another transacts business or handles money or property not his own; such relationship implies great confidence and trust in the person's financial honesty.

FRAUD: IN THE INDUCEMENT: A material misrepresentation of fact designed to get a person to enter into a contract or other agreement. The victim may defend himself in a suit on the contract by proving that fraud caused him to enter into it.

FREEHOLD: An interest in real estate not less than an estate for life.

GOODWILL: The economic advantage over competitors which a business has acquired by virtue of habitual patronage of customers.

HEREDITAMENTS: The largest classification of property; including lands, tenements, and incorporeal property, such as rights of way and future interests.

INJUNCTION: A writ or order issued under the seal of the court to restrain one or more parties to a suit from doing an act which is deemed to be inequitable or unjust in regard to the rights of some other party or parties in the suit or proceeding.

INSTRUMENT: A written legal document created to effect the rights of the parties.

INTEGRATION: In a written contract, the piece of paper on which the parties settle as the definitive expression of the terms of the contract. It is not essential to the existence of a contract.

IRREVOCABLE: Incapable of being recalled or revoked; unchangeable, unalterable.

LAND CONTRACT: An executory (unperformed on either side) contract for the purchase of real property under the terms of which legal title to the property is retained by the vendor until such time as all conditions stated in the contract have been fulfilled. It is commonly used for the purchase of real estate on the installment plan.

LEASE: A contract whereby, for a consideration, usually termed rent, one who is entitled to the possession of real property transfers such rights to another for life, for a term, or at will.

LEASEHOLD: The estate or interest which a lessee of real estate has therein by virtue of his lease.

LIABILITY: Any debt or legal obligation. Also used to include the obligations, legal and equitable, or a business entity to its owners as well as its creditors.

LIEN: A legal right or claim upon a specific property or asset which attaches to the asset until a debt is satisfied.

LITIGATION: The act of carrying on a lawsuit.

MEETING OF THE MINDS: Whenever all parties to a contract agree to the exact terms thereof.

MINOR: A person under an age specified by law, usually 21. Contracts made by such persons cannot be enforced against them unless a minor affirms the contract when he attains his majority.

MORATORIUM: An emergency act by a legislative body to suspend the legal enforcement of contractual obligations.

MORTGAGE: An instrument in writing, duly executed and delivered, that creates a lien upon real estate as security for the payment of a specified debt, which is usually in the form of a bond. A mortgage taken out on a chattel is given the name chattel mortgage.

MORTGAGEE: The party who lends money and takes a mortgage to secure the payment thereof.

MORTGAGOR: A person who borrows money and gives a mortgage on his property as security for the payment of the debt.

OPTION: A right given for a consideration to acquire an interest in goods or property; the right is given on specified conditions for a stated period of time, and if is not exercised in accordance with these restrictions, it lapses; if it is properly exercised, the grantor of the option must perform.

PAROL CONTRACT: An unwritten contract, one formed by oral agreement of the parties. Certain categories of these agreements cannot be enforced because of the Statute of Frauds (q.v.).

PERFORMANCE: Fulfillment of a contract or promise, or any kind of legal obligation according to the terms included in it.

PERSONAL PROPERTY: Any property which is not real property.

POWER OF ATTORNEY: A written instrument duly signed and executed on behalf of an owner of property, of a business, or of a claim for money, which authorizes an agent to act on behalf of the owner to the extent indicated in the instrument.

PRINCIPAL: The employer of an agent hired to do business with third persons; also a person for whose debts and liabilities a surety is responsible.

QUIT CLAIM DEED: A deed which conveys simply the grantor's rights or interest in real estate, without any agreement or covenant as to the nature or extent of that interest, or any other covenants; usually used to relieve the grantor of liability for defects in the title he has in the land he is conveying.

RATIFICATION: The process of acceptance by which a voidable agreement becomes enforceable.

REAL PROPERTY: Land, and generally whatever is erected thereupon or affixed thereto.

RECEIVER: A person appointed by a court to manage property owned by an insolvent debtor until the claims of creditors have been met, or to manage property involved in a lawsuit pending its outcome.

RELEASE: The act or writing by which some claim or interest is surrendered to another person.

REMEDY: The means by which a right is enforced or by which the violation of a right is prevented.

RENT: The compensation paid for the use of real estate.

REVOCATION: An act of recalling a power of authority conferred, as with the revocation of the power of accepting an offer of a contract.

SALES CONTRACT: A contract by which the buyer and seller agree to terms of sale.

SPECIFIC PERFORMANCE: A remedy in a court of equity compelling a defendant to carry out the terms of an agreement or contract.

STATUTE OF FRAUDS: State law which provides that certain contracts must be in writing to be enforceable at law. Among the classes of contract covered are contracts which cannot be completed within a year, contracts for the sale of an interest in land, and contracts for the sale of goods, unless some of the goods or payment money has been transferred.

SUBLETTING: A leasing by a tenant to another, who holds under the tenant.

SUBROGATION: A doctrine in equity which gives a party aggrieved by a second party, the rights that a third person has against the second party.

SURETY: One who guarantees the performance of another.

SURRENDER: The cancellation of a lease by mutual consent of lessor and lessee.

TORT: A wrongful act which violates a general legal right of another person; i.e., a right which, unlike a contract right, does not arise from a specific agreement of the wrongdoer and the wronged person.

TORTFEASOR: A person who commits a tort.

TORTIOUS: Wrongful.

UNCONSCIONABLE CONTRACT OR CLAUSE: A contract or clause thereof which cannot be enforced because one of the parties to the contract used a greatly superior bargaining position to impose unduly harsh terms on the other.

UNILATERAL CONTRACT: A contract involving performance of an act by one party and a promise of compensation by the other; e.g. a reward for finding a lost item.

VALID: Having force or binding force; legally sufficient and authorized by law.

VOID: To have no force or effect; that which is completely unenforceable.

VOIDABLE: That which is capable of being adjudged void but which may become enforceable if ratified by proper action.

WAIVER: The renunciation, abandonment, or surrender of some claim, right, or priviledge.

WARRANTY DEED: A conveyance of land in which the grantor warrants the title to the grantee.

WRITING: The term, "a writing" signifies a document, either written or printed, as opposed to the spoken word.

Index